GUERRILLA WARFARE

GUERRILLA WARFARE

Editor:
JOHN PIMLOTT

THE MILITARY PRESS

New York

A Bison Book

This edition is published by The Military Press, distributed by Crown Publishers Inc.

Printed in Hong Kong

Library of Congress Cataloging in Publication Data
Guerrilla warfare.
  "A Bison book."
  1. Guerrilla warfare—History—20th century.
2. Military history, Modern—20th century.
I. Pimlott, John.
U240.G8238   1985   355'.02184   85-5017

ISBN 0-517-451395

h g f e d c b a

LIST OF CONTRIBUTORS

JOHN PIMLOTT is a Senior Lecturer in the Department of War Studies and International Affairs at The Royal Military Academy Sandhurst. His books include *B-29 Superfortress*, *Battle of the Bulge*, *Vietnam: The history and the tactics*, *The Middle East Conflicts*, *British Military Operations, 1945-84* and (with Ian Beckett) *Armed Forces and Modern Counter-Insurgency*. He is also consultant editor to the *War in Peace* part-work.

IAN BECKETT is a Senior Lecturer in the Department of War Studies and International Affairs at The Royal Military Academy Sandhurst. He is author of *Politicians and Defence*, *Riflemen Form*, *A Nation in Arms* and (with John Pimlott) *Armed Forces and Modern Counter-Insurgency* and has contributed to *British Military Operations, 1945-84* and the *War in Peace* part-work. (Chapter 1)

DAVID JOHNSON was a Senior Lecturer in the Department of War Studies and International Affairs at The Royal Military Academy Sandhurst until 1984. He has contributed to the *War in Peace* part-work and specializes in aspects of international politics and terrorism. (Chapter 6)

NIGEL DE LEE is a Senior Lecturer in the Department of War Studies and International Affairs at The Royal Military Academy Sandhurst. He specializes in Far Eastern and Northern European affairs and was editor of *The Chinese War Machine*. (Chapter 2)

PETER REED was educated at a British provincial university and is a freelance writer who specializes in modern military affairs. He has contributed to various journals and to *British Military Operations, 1945-84*. (Chapter 4)

FRANCIS TOASE is a Senior Lecturer in the Department of War Studies and International Affairs at The Royal Military Academy Sandhurst. He has contributed to *British Military Operations, 1945-84*, *Armed Forces and Modern Counter-Insurgency* and the *War in Peace* part-work. (Chapter 3)

Page 1: A member of Yassir Arafat's Fatah bodyguard safeguards Arafat's hideout.
Page 2-3: British soldiers with full riot-control equipment in Belfast.
Page 4-5: Portuguese troops land by helicopter to counter Paigg guerrillas, Angola.

CONTENTS

Goya's *Los fusilamientos del 3 de Mayo* shows the French invaders executing Spanish resisters.

1. THE TRADITION

Much confusion surrounds the definition of guerrilla warfare, which is best described as being 'an irregular war carried on by small bodies of men acting independently.' Most confusion arises from the development, since 1945, of revolutionary guerrilla warfare or insurgency which has implied a politico-military campaign waged by guerrillas with the object of overthrowing the government of a state. This, however, disguises the fact that guerrilla warfare is essentially only a tactical method which is applicable to many different forms of military conflict. In essence, the modern revolutionary guerrilla has merely added political, social, economic and psychological elements to traditional irregular military tactics. Prior to 1945 guerrilla warfare rarely had such revolutionary intent and was understood more in terms of irregulars operating against an opponent's army or lines of communication in support of conventional military operations or, alternatively, in terms of a general insurrection against an occupying army. As interpreted prior to 1945, guerrilla warfare is perhaps more properly defined as partisan warfare.

As a tactical method, guerrilla warfare has a long antecedence, the earliest documented reference being in the Hittite *Anastas Papyrus* dating from the fifteenth century BC. Similarly, the actual minutiae of guerrilla tactics portrayed in Mao Tse-tung's celebrated work, *On Protracted War*, first published in 1937, is not recognizably different from the tactics described by the ancient Chinese military theorist, Sun Tzu, whose *Art of War* dates from around the fifth century BC. As far as the Western world is concerned, the Bible is not short of references to guerrilla warfare, notably the irregular tactics utilized by the followers of Judas Maccabaeus against the Syrians in 166 BC (as described in the Book of Daniel in the Old Testament and in the first and second Books of Maccabees in the Apocrypha). Much Roman military history is a catalogue of irregular warfare in North Africa, Spain, Britain, Germany and Gaul. From the Middle Ages come yet further examples including: the wars of the Welsh against the English so vividly described in the work of the twelfth century Welsh

Above: The Tyrolean patriot Josef Speckbacher led the Tyrolean peasant army in the Inn Valley against French and Bavarian troops in 1809.

scholar, Giraldus Cambrensis; the harassing raids of the Constable of France, Bertrand du Guesclin, against the English in the closing stages of the Hundred Years' War; or the numerous peasant uprisings of central and eastern Europe.

To a large extent, such irregular warfare was either the natural resort of primitive peoples faced with a more sophisticated opponent, or a resort of the weak against the strong. On occasions, too, it was merely brigandage which acquired the status of legend as in the sagas of the Haiduks and the Klephs, both Balkan Christian groups opposed to Turkish rule in the seventeenth and eighteenth centuries, or, for that matter, the Robin Hood of Medieval England. Increasingly, however, while not ceasing to be a resort of the weak or the oppressed, it was appreciated that guerrilla warfare might play a role in a wider conventional conflict. By the eighteenth century many European armies were experimenting with irregular troops and light infantry, with both eastern Europe and the Americas providing ready proving grounds. The Indian wars in the American colonies and Canada had already provided many examples of irregular successes, such as the defeat of the British force commanded by Major General Edward Braddock in 1755. During the American War of Independence (1775-83), however, partisans operated successfully on both sides in

Above: Men of Banastre Tarleton's British Legion, the American Loyalist unit he led with distinction during the American War of Independence.
Right: The Duke of Wellington at the Battle of Salamanca, 22 July 1812. Without the British Army, Spanish guerrillas would have been ineffective.

support of conventional operations. This was especially true in the Southern states such as North and South Carolina and a number of talented partisan leaders emerged, such as the British officers Banastre Tarleton and Patrick Ferguson, and the Americans, Thomas Sumter and Francis 'Swamp Fox' Marion. Indeed, the tactics utilized by partisans and light infantry in America spawned some of the first modern texts to deal specifically with the opportunities for irregular warfare. Thus two Hessians, Johann von Ewald and Andreas Emmerich, who had both fought with the British Army in America, published works on the subject in 1785 and 1789 respectively.

These pioneering works were followed by still others, which derived their experience not from America but from Europe for, at the close of the eighteenth century, the nature of warfare itself was utterly transformed by the outbreak of the French Revolution and by the French Revolutionary and Napoleonic wars that followed. In seeking to defend their newly won liberties, in August

Above: The Duke of Wellington's army crossing the Pyrenees, 1813. Left: Goya's *La Carga de Los Mamelucos en la Puerta del sol* shows Spaniards resisting the French.

1793 the French Committee of Public Safety instituted the *levée en masse*, by which all able-bodied Frenchmen were literally conscripted overnight to serve as a 'nation in arms.' Driven by patriotic nationalism, the new French citizen armies swept across Europe. Defeat at the hands of the French ultimately engendered a national response to the challenge of the Revolution. In Prussia, this took the form of emulating the French concept of a 'nation in arms,' while elsewhere it amounted to nationalist uprisings against French occupation. There were, in fact, a number of these uprisings. The part of western France known as La Vendée rose in revolt against the Republicans between 1793 and 1796, which resulted in a bitterly contested struggle by the *Chouans*, as the Vendéans were known. Andreas Hofer led the Tyrol into revolt against the Napoleonic Empire in 1809 while, further afield, the Haitians rose in revolt on Santo Domingo under the leadership of Toussaint L'Ouverture, compelling Napoleon to dispatch an army of 30,000 men under General Leclerc there in 1802. The best known and ultimately the most successful uprising was that in Spain, from which the word 'guerrilla' derives, meaning literally 'little war.'

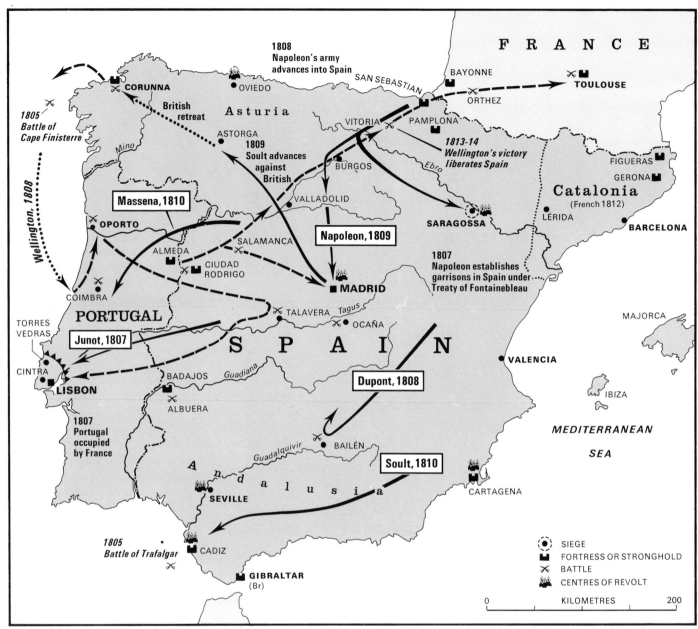

F R A N C E

1808
Napoleon's army
advances into Spain

1805
Battle of
Cape Finisterre

CORUNNA

OVIEDO

British
retreat

Asturia

SAN SEBASTIAN

BAYONNE

ORTHEZ

TOULOUSE

×

ASTORGA

1809
Soult advances
against
British

VITORIA

PAMPLONA

1813-14
Wellington's victory
liberates Spain

Mino

BURGOS

Ebro

FIGUERAS

GERONA

Massena, 1810

VALLADOLID

Catalonia
(French 1812)

OPORTO

SALAMANCA

Napoleon, 1809

SARAGOSSA

LÉRIDA

BARCELONA

ALMEDA

CIUDAD
RODRIGO

COIMBRA

MADRID

1807
Napoleon establishes
garrisons in Spain under
Treaty of Fontainebleau

PORTUGAL

TALAVERA

Tagus

OCAÑA

S P A I N

MAJORCA

TORRES
VEDRAS

Junot, 1807

Dupont, 1808

VALENCIA

CINTRA

LISBON

BADAJOS

Guadiana

IBIZA

ALBUERA

BAILÉN

Soult, 1810

MEDITERRANEAN
SEA

1807
Portugal
occupied
by France

Guadalquivir

A n d a l u s i a

CARTAGENA

SEVILLE

1805
Battle of Trafalgar

CADIZ

GIBRALTAR
(Br)

SIEGE

FORTRESS OR STRONGHOLD

BATTLE

CENTRES OF REVOLT

0   KILOMETRES   200

Wellington, 1808

Guerrilla resistance in Spain was the product of military defeat and occupation. In accordance with a secret treaty concluded between the French and the *de facto* ruler of Spain, the royal favorite Manuel de Godoy, French troops began to enter Spain in September 1807. Ostensibly the French were *en route* to conquer Portugal, which Napoleon wished to ensure adhered to the Berlin Decrees of November 1806. The Decrees were designed to exclude British trade from continental Europe and enforce an economic blockade on Napoleon's sole surviving enemy, all other European states being either under French occupation or acquiescent in French domination. Spain was also

technically a party to this 'continental system'; Godoy was in French pay and a Spanish corps of 15,000 troops was stationed in northern Germany as part of the French Army in order to guarantee Spanish co-operation. It is clear, however, that Napoleon did not fully trust Godoy and, harboring ambitions to control the Spanish Fleet and Spain's overseas colonies, seized the opportunity given him to further his aims by the confused nature of internal Spanish politics. In February 1808 the French troops in Spain took possession of key points, although many others were already occupied by French troops and had been since the previous autumn. Both the Spanish King and his heir were

Above: Spanish guerrillas.
Left: The Peninsular War, 1807-1814, and the centers of resistance.
Below left: Francisco Espoz y Mina, the best known Spanish guerrilla leader.

then maneuvered into abdicating in May 1808 and Napoleon's own brother, Joseph, installed on the Spanish throne in July. Almost as soon as the King had abdicated, spontaneous risings occurred in Madrid and many provincial areas with the initiative being seized by so-called provincial juntas such as those in Valencia, the Asturias and Seville. A Central Junta was formed in September 1808 but lacked real authority and the Seville Junta invited Britain to come to Spain's assistance. Initially the forces raised by the juntas and the Spanish Army performed reasonably well, including the corps in Germany which was spirited away by the Royal Navy and repatriated. A small French garrison was forced to capitulate at Bailén in July 1808 and a British force, landed in Portugal under the command of Sir Arthur Wellesley, triumphed over the

French at Rolica and Vimeiro. However, Wellesley's superiors threw away the fruits of victory through the Convention of Cintra and Napoleon himself took command of 270,000 troops in November 1808. The Spanish armies were routed and a British army led by Sir John Moore was driven from Corunna in January 1809.

Napoleon, however, had miscalculated in believing that his original force of some 80,000 men was sufficient to pacify Spain and he now miscalculated again in believing that the 'Spanish business' was concluded. Guerrilla groups or *partides* first began to appear in Galicia and Aragon and by 1810 had swelled into four 'armies' based in the north, in Catalonia, Galicia, the Asturias and Valencia. Many of the bands were a spontaneous response to occupation while others were based upon traditional militias such as the Miqueletes and Somaten of Catalonia. To a large extent resistance came from the lower elements of society, since many enlightened Spanish liberals supported the French presence as a means of political transformation and some 12,000 Spanish collaborators left Spain with the retreating French armies in 1813-14.

Many of the guerrilla leaders were thus men of humble origin such as the Castillian peasant Juan Martin Diaz, known as 'El Empecinado' ('The Stubborn One'), who began his guerrilla career by ambushing French couriers in March 1808. Diaz was briefly detained by the Spanish authorities in November 1808 but escaped and continued to evade the operations directed against him by the French Generals Hugo and Guye in the Madrid and Salamanca areas. In the process his band grew from an initial strength of 48 men to some 1400 by 1811. Other notable guerrilla leaders included: Juan Palarea ('El Medico'), who operated in the area between Upper La Mancha and Toledo and whose successes included the capture of the French Colonel Lejeune on a mission for Joseph in April 1811; Juan Diaz Porlier ('El Marquesito'), who operated in the Asturias with the assistance of a British naval squadron and in August 1811 drove the French garrison from the city of Santander before retiring; Jean de Mendietta ('El Capuchino'), who

operated in Zamora and captured the French General Franceschi-Delonne in May 1809; and Francisco Espoz y Mina, a farmer's son from Navarre. Mina assumed command of a guerrilla band in March 1810 after its original leader, his nephew, had been captured. Like Diaz, Mina presided over a substantial growth in the numbers of his followers from some 400 men in 1810 to over 7000 by 1813. Named as Commander General of Navarre in April 1810, Mina eliminated potential rivals and continually evaded the local French commanders including General Abbé. Among his successes was the destruction of a French convoy guarded by 2000 troops in April 1812.

Much of Spain was ideal guerrilla terrain in which the guerrillas enjoyed a large measure of popular support although, in some areas, intimidation of an apathetic population undoubtedly occurred. The guerrillas also possessed superior mobility and superior local knowledge to the French. The French responded by employing 20 squadrons of gendarmerie to guard the main route from Bayonne to Madrid and by building wooden blockhouses at suitable intervals. The French were also forced to disperse large numbers of troops throughout the countryside, so much so that Marshal Bessiéres complained in 1811 that he could not concentrate even 10,000 men for fear of having his supply lines cut and large amounts of territory overrun by the guerrillas. The experience of the French is well described in the memoirs of de Rocca, a French Hussar officer who wrote an account of his operations against the guerrillas:

The garrisons which they [the French] had left on the military roads to keep the country in check, were constantly attacked; they were obliged to construct little citadels for their safety. . . . In the plains, the posts of communication fortified one or two of the houses at the entrance of each village, for safety during the night, or as a place of retreat when attacked. . . . The French soldiers thus shut up in their little fortresses, frequently heard the gay sounds of the guitars of their enemies, who came to pass their nights in the neighboring villages, where they were always well received and feasted by the inhabitants. The French armies could only obtain provisions and ammunition under

convoy of very strong detachments, which were for ever harassed and frequently intercepted. . . . The French could only maintain themselves in Spain by terror; they were constantly under the necessity of punishing the innocent with the guilty, and of taking revenge on the weak for the offenses of the powerful.

There is little doubt that such guerrilla action had an important impact upon French morale and also furnished the British Army under the Duke of Wellington with Intelligence through the interception of French couriers, whose dispatches could sometimes be deciphered.

It is important to recognize that while Wellington's small army derived considerable advantages from the inability of the French to concentrate against it for fear of losing control of territory to the guerrillas, the Spanish guerrillas could not have survived without substantial British logistic support. Nor could they have survived without the additional military pressure on the French from the British Army and its regular Portuguese and Spanish allies. It

was Wellington's Army rather than the estimated 30,000 guerrillas who ultimately liberated Spain. As a whole, the campaigns in Spain probably detained some 275,000 French and satellite troops at any one time and may have cost between 180,000 and 300,000 French casualties in five years. Perhaps more important, from the point of view of the Spanish, was that the guerrillas had enabled Spain to claim some part in its own deliverance. That had an important psychological effect on the people and was ultimately to contribute to a struggle between liberals and absolutists that took place in Spain after liberation. A number of the guerrilla leaders were, in fact, executed during that struggle, including Diaz, Porlier and Mendietta.

Such national uprisings as those in Spain and the Tyrol, together with the successes of Russian irregulars in harrying the French armies in Russia in 1812, brought further contributions to irregular warfare theory in the years that followed Napoleon's fall in 1815. Among those who devoted volumes specifically to irregular warfare were the Prussians, George Wilhelm von Valentini (1799)

and Carl von Decker (1821), the Frenchman, Le Miere de Corvey (1823), and the Russian, Denis Davidov (1841). Theorists of general war such as Baron Henri Jomini and Karl von Clausewitz also devoted some attention to guerrilla war, but all these authors, as well as two Polish theorists, Wojciech Chrzanowski (1835) and Karol Bogumir Stolzman (1844), primarily examined the value of the partisan in the context of a conventional war in support of conventional operations. In later years there were some further examples of guerrilla or irregular tactics being used in such struggles as the Greek War of Independence (1821-1827), the Italian Risorgimento (1848-1871), and the American Civil War (1861-1865), the last of which featured notable irregular cavalry leaders such as the Confederates John Singleton Mosby and Nathan Bedford Forrest. However, the more usual pattern of events in nineteenth-century

An idealized view of a British action in the South African War. In reality, the Boers invariably melted away before the British could come to grips.

Europe was either that of the brief, generally unsuccessful urban insurrection such as the widespread uprisings which occurred in 1830 and 1848, or short conventional wars such as those fought by Prussia against Denmark (1864), Austria (1866) and France (1870). Although socialists like Friedrich Engels, Karl Marx or, later, Lenin were disposed to seek lessons in urban risings such as the disastrous affair of the Paris Commune (1871), mainstream military thought was concerned only with conventional war in Europe.

Yet European armies were increasingly confronted with irregular warfare in their expanding colonial empires. The kind of opponents met were astonishingly varied in characteristics and methods. In the case of the British Army, for example, opponents varied from conventionally trained armies such as the Sikhs (1845-1846, 1848-1849) and Egyptians (1882) to disciplined but unsophisticated foes such as the Zulus (1879) and Matabele (1893, 1896). In addition, there were genuine guerrilla opponents such as the dacoits of Burma (1885-1892) and the Maoris of New Zealand (1846-1847, 1860-1861, 1863-1866). Unlike most other guerrilla opponents, the Boers (1881, 1899-1902) were of European origin and were mounted. Europeans were usually successful against native armies through superior technology and firepower; many campaigns were fought more against the terrain than the enemy. But this was not invariably true and European armies met with disasters, too, such as the British defeats at Isandhlwana (1879) and Maiwand (1880) and the overwhelming catastrophe that befell an Italian army at Adowa (1896) in Abyssinia.

Many European armies evolved their own methods of dealing with colonial warfare. The British in particular adopted a sophisticated pacification strategy against the Boers during the later stages of the South African War (1899-1902). This involved the constant harassment of Boer commandos by mobile British columns and the steady restriction of the Boers' ability to maneuver by the liberal use of barbed wire and blockhouses allied to the systematic destruction of Boer farms and

livestock and the detention of Boer families to deny support for those in the field. However experiences in the colonies were so diverse that little coherent doctrine developed. The celebrated British manual, C E Callwell's *Small Wars: Their Principles and Practise*, appeared only in 1896. Callwell's approach to guerrilla war, which he recognized as being 'a harassing form of warfare ... most difficult to bring to a satisfactory conclusion,' was primarily military. Similarly, the US Army did not develop any coherent counterguerrilla doctrine from its campaigns against Mexicans, Indians and Filipinos. The one exception to this primarily military approach was that of the French, whose campaigns in Indochina, Madagascar and Morocco in the second half of the nineteenth century resulted in the development of progressive pacification – the slow methodical expansion of French administration hand-in-hand with their military presence like a *tache d'huile* (oil slick). Indeed, the French essentially applied *tache d'huile* strategy in their campaigns against the Viet Minh in Indochina between 1946 and 1954, an indication of how far European armies tended to cling to strategies and tactics that had worked in the past in the belief that guerrilla warfare had not intrinsically changed.

Above: General Christiaan Beyers, a Boer commander noted for 'praying and pillage.'
Top: Last Stand of the 66th Foot at the battle of Maiwand, 27 July 1880, in the 2nd Afghan War. Superior technology did not guarantee victory.
Top right: A Boer commando on Spion Kop, 1900. Skilled marksmen and horsemen, Boers were formidable foes.
Far right: Tribesmen of the North West Frontier of India, c 1879.
Right: Louis Botha and his son, c 1900.

Rather similarly, in the 1930s British manuals on counterinsurgency tended to dwell on traditional 'imperial policing,' seeking examples in colonial uprisings such as the disturbances in Cyprus in 1931 or those inspired by Arab unrest in Palestine between 1936 and 1937. The problem was that guerrilla warfare doctrine was changing. One significant signpost to the future was the experience of T E Lawrence, whose *Revolt in the Desert* (1927) and *Seven Pillars of Wisdom* (1935), if not always accurate as history, were the first modern works clearly to articulate principles of guerrilla warfare which transcended the purely tactical. As a guerrilla leader, Lawrence was not particularly outstanding and certainly not the equal of the German general, Paul von Lettow-Vorbeck, who skillfully defended German East Africa against vastly superior Allied forces from November 1914 until

he surrendered upon hearing of the German capitulation in Europe four years later.

An enigmatic figure, Lawrence had become interested in the Arab world as an archeologist and, through his knowledge of the area, was attached to British Intelligence in Cairo in December 1914 following Turkey's entry into World War I in alliance with the Central Powers of Imperial Germany and Austria-Hungary. Although he had suggested stirring up Turkey's Arab population, the 'Arab Revolt' against Turkey's Ottoman Empire began without Lawrence's intervention in June 1916. The Arabs were nominally led by the Sherif of Mecca, ibn-Ali Hussein, but Lawrence was able to make contact with one of Hussein's sons, Feisal, who was believed to be the Arab most likely to succeed in uniting his people. Lawrence was sent to liaise with Feisal in December 1916; he

Left: T E Lawrence in Arab garb, photographed at Aqaba which fell to the Arab forces on 6 July 1917. Lawrence then carried the news to Cairo.
Right: Feisal with his Ageyl bodyguard. After World War I he became King of Mesopotamia (Syria) and subsequently of Iraq. His brother, Abdullah, became emir of Transjordan (Jordan).
Below: Representatives of Arab tribes coming in under a White Flag to swear allegiance to Sheikh Feisal at Aqaba, 1917.

Members of one of Lawrence's railroad raiding parties.

took part in his first raid in January 1917 and assisted in the unsuccessful attack on a train in March 1917. Although there were other British officers attached to the Arab forces who were superior in rank, Lawrence had Feisal's confidence and he increasingly accompanied Arab parties on raids. It would appear that he was instrumental in persuading the Arabs to capture Aqaba; Lawrence set out from Wejh on 9 May 1917 with the Arab forces, and they paused to sabotage the Turkish Hejaz railroad *en route*. Lawrence's precise role in the fall of Aqaba is, however, problematical, notably in the important action at Aba el Lisari which preceded the fall of the town on 6 July 1917. Lawrence himself carried the news to Cairo and, having met the British commander, General Sir Edmund Allenby, thereafter co-ordinated the Arab guerrillas in support of the British advance toward Damascus, which fell in October 1918. Lawrence was increasingly involved in the morass of Allied political intrigue in the Middle East and after the war he sought personal refuge in the ranks of first the RAF and then the Tank Corps. He was then allowed to return to the RAF but, within weeks of his final discharge in 1935, was killed in a motorcycle accident.

In essence, the Arab Revolt was a sideshow in a subsidiary theater of war, although it has been calculated that some 3000 Arabs tied down up to 50,000 Turkish troops. Its real importance derives from Lawrence's account of it, insignificant though the campaign actually was in terms of the war as a whole. It is true that Lawrence appears to be an original theorist because he had no literary competitors among other practitioners of guerrilla warfare at the time, but there have been few better descriptions of guerrilla conflict. To Lawrence, the Arab guerrillas represented 'an influence ... an idea, a thing invulnerable, intangible, without front or back, drifting about like gas.' By contrast, the Turkish troops were confined to garrisons and static lines of communication:

Armies were like plants, immobile as a whole, firm rooted through long stems to the head. We might be a vapour, blowing where we listed. Our kingdoms lay in each man's mind, and as we wanted nothing material to live on, so perhaps we offered nothing to the killing. It seemed a Regular soldier might be helpless without a target, owning only what he sat on, and subjugating only what, by order, he could poke his rifle at.

Beyond the obvious lessons of highly mobile nomadic forces attacking Turkish communications and avoiding Turkish garrisons and thus offsetting much larger enemy numbers through mobility, Lawrence also stressed the moral and propaganda aspects of guerrilla war. Thus, 'We had won a province when we had taught the civilians in it to die for our ideal of freedom.'

Other writers also connected popular struggle or a 'people's war' to guerrilla tactics, most notably Lenin, but it should be recognized that Lenin regarded guerrilla war merely as a substitute for adequate conventional strength and only one of several tools that might be employed by revolutionaries to achieve power. His actual contribution to guerrilla warfare derives more from the organizational weapon of a monolithic party structure as the instrument for organizing the proletariat in their struggle. But if one is to search for signposts for the future of guerrilla war, far more significant than the thought of either Lawrence or Lenin is the practical conduct of the guerrilla war in Ireland between 1919 and 1921. Just as Lawrence and Lenin both inspired Mao Tse-tung to some extent so later writers, notably George Grivas who led EOKA in Cyprus in the 1950s, drew inspiration and lessons from the Irish Republican Army (IRA).

In many respects the IRA campaign was a precursor of the highly politically motivated guerrilla campaigns to be fought after 1945, although it should be noted that many IRA units were far less effective than has sometimes been claimed and by no means entirely in concert with the population whom they claimed to represent. The attacks upon the substantial but unfortified police houses, euphemistically known as 'barracks,' in 1920-21 were not so much a carefully calculated political campaign to destroy the Royal Irish Constabulary (RIC) but rather a response to the fact that they were easy targets. Similarly, although quicker than the British to recognize the importance of Intelligence, the IRA's Intelligence network was not as efficient as supposed at the time; if anything, the IRA became more and more bureaucratized during the course of the campaign and consequent-

Above: Eamonn De Valera speaking at Los Angeles in 1919. De Valera headed Sinn Fein from 1917 to 1926.

Below: A procession in Shaftesbury Square, Belfast, 1920. The realities of Ulster Loyalism led to the partition of Ireland in 1921.

Above: Sir Carson, leader of the Ulster Protestants, addressing an anti-Home Rule meeting in September 1913.

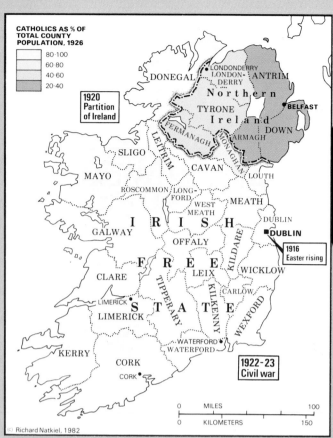

CATHOLICS AS % OF
TOTAL COUNTY
POPULATION, 1926

80-100
60-80
40-60
20-40

DONEGAL
LONDONDERRY
LONDON-
DERRY
ANTRIM
Northern
TYRONE
Ireland
BELFAST
FERMANAGH
DOWN
MONAGHAN
ARMAGH
SLIGO
LEITRIM
CAVAN
MAYO
LOUTH
ROSCOMMON
LONG-
FORD
WEST
MEATH
MEATH
GALWAY
DUBLIN
DUBLIN
OFFALY
KILDARE
WICKLOW
CLARE
LEIX
TIPPERARY
CARLOW
KILKENNY
LIMERICK
WEXFORD
LIMERICK
KERRY
WATERFORD
WATERFORD
CORK
CORK

IRISH FREE STATE

1920
Partition
of Ireland

1916
Easter rising

1922-23
Civil war

0   MILES   100
0   KILOMETERS   150

(c) Richard Natkiel, 1982

19 CASH SUPPLY STORES

Far left: The division of Ireland as a result of the 'Troubles.'
Left: British troops facing crowds in Dublin, February 1921. The troops were ill-trained for such a role.
Bottom left: Suspects held at pistol point by auxiliaries of the RIC, 1920.
Bottom: Sinn Fein delegates, London, October 1921. Seated third left is Michael Collins, IRA Intelligence Chief; he was killed in an ambush in 1922.
Below: Irish refugees from Belfast in Dublin, June 1922. Sectarianism was always a feature of conflict in Ireland.

ly suffered its own defeats at the hands of British Intelligence. Thus the IRA was rarely able to take on more than a platoon of British troops at any one time and was as ready for a settlement as the British by 1921. Indeed, it could be argued that the campaign succeeded largely because of the lack of political direction on the British side, the ill-defined role of a largely untrained British Army (which always lacked sufficient manpower and transport), and the mistaken use of British ex-servicemen as auxiliaries to the RIC. Nevertheless, Ireland did provide lessons for the future that should have been noted.

As already indicated, however, what lessons there were to learn from Ireland were ignored by British theorists in the interwar period and it is perhaps equally significant that one of the most important syntheses of military theory to appear at this time – *Makers of Modern Strategy*, published in the United States in 1943 – devoted but four of over 500 pages to the subject of guerrilla warfare theory. Yet, at the very moment that the book was being published, guerrilla warfare had once more assumed considerable importance, this time in World War II, where the German occupation of much of Europe and the Japanese occupation of much of Southeast Asia had provoked popular resistance.

Resistance, of course, took many forms and developed at different times in different occupied countries. In some senses it could be seen as an extension of prewar politics in Europe, since many European societies had become increasingly politicized in the interwar years and there had been both polarization and virtual political warfare before the war broke out. In the Far East it could be seen as an expression of latent nationalism that had been nurtured under colonial rule long before the Japanese provided a catalyst. Defeat of the Allies was naturally likely to bring at least a temporary shock and only gradually did people become aware of the consequences of that defeat and inclined toward overt resistance. It could begin simply as unspoken thoughts or gestures such as refusing to purchase German newspapers, defacing posters, or listening to the BBC, before escalating to hiding Allied servicemen, running clan-

destine newspapers or taking part in demonstrations. Beyond that it might develop into open sabotage or full-time guerrilla struggle. Much would depend upon the terrain – in states like Denmark it was clearly impossible for resisters to organize as full-time guerrilla groups, whereas it could be done in the Massif Central of France, the mountains of Greece and Yugoslavia, the forests and marshes of Russia, and the jungles of Malaya or the Philippines. Much could also depend upon the availability of former members of the armed forces or regular troops cut off by a German or Japanese advance. Much, too, could depend upon the occupation policies of the conquerors; the French resistance was considerably boosted by the German introduction of forced labor in the summer of 1943, resulting in a 14-fold increase in the number of attacks on German installations that year as compared to 1942.

Just as the kind of resistance varied, so did the participants in resistance vary. Virtually all classes were to be found both in the resistance and in the ranks of collaborators. In a sense every individual was faced with a choice at one time or another and some unexpected decisions were made. In France, for example, some strong anti-fascists of the prewar years took up the struggle but others collaborated. A searching critic of the prewar Right like Jeanson of the newspaper *Aujourd'hui* could become a collaborator. In states like Yugoslavia, collaborators and resisters could vary with ethnicity. Draza Mihailovich's Cetniks in Yugoslavia were principally Montenegrin and Serbian as well as being strongly royalist in sympathy and anti-communist. By the middle of the war the Cetniks were collaborating with the Italians. Tito's communist guerrillas were, by comparison, primarily Croats and Slovenes. Still other Croats, known as *Ustashas*, fought with the Germans. In other countries the politics of resistance could also be extremely varied, with some nationalists fighting the invaders but others (such as many nationalists in Norway and the Netherlands) fighting with the German Army in Russia. Similarly, many prewar Asian nationalists co-operated with the Japanese, who sponsored organizations such as the Indian National Army. In Greece both nationalists and communists fought against the Germans but, as in Yugoslavia, they also fought each other, a civil war between the royalist EDES and the communist ELAS erupting in December 1944. The role of the communists in particular has been the subject of much debate, mostly surrounding the question of whether or not they supported the Nazi-Soviet Pact of 1939 and only attempted to resist after the German invasion of Russia in 1941 or were drawn into the war against the Nazis much earlier.

Resistance as a more overt activity could also be extremely varied. One aspect was the gathering of Intelligence. It was, of course, one of the principal means by which the Allies could build up a picture of the order of battle of German or Japanese forces. Virtually anyone could count troops, or the funnels of a ship, or estimate the size of a gun with reasonable accuracy. Other valuable information included, in Europe, industrial plans and production figures, timetables and the results of air raids, and even relatively minor information such as the times of curfew could assist Allied agents dropped into occupied countries. Another aspect was the assistance given to Allied personnel, especially aircrew, to evade capture. Some 10,309 evaders and 25,208 Allied prisoners of war escaped from Western Europe during the war, although this included a large number who simply walked out of Italian camps when Italy capitulated in September 1943. Yet another method of effective resistance was the attitude of affable incompetence adopted by the Czechs, which infuriated their conquerors, and further passive resistance was the highly effective strike of the majority of Norway's schoolteachers in protest against the introduction of a fascist syllabus. Some clandestine newspapers attained quite astonishing circulations. In one six-month period a printing press at Drinici in Yugoslavia produced over 2,000,000 pages of propaganda material.

In theory, the most effective form of resistance was direct subversion. This could also vary from a man wielding a hammer in a factory production line to large-scale guerrilla operations. It might

include the use of explosives, as in the destruction of the railroad bridge over the Gorgopotamos gorge in Greece in 1942 or the destruction of the German heavy-water plant at Vemork in Norway in 1943 or the massed sabotage of German communications in France a year before D-Day. Secondly, subversion could include actual attacks on German troops but much, as already indicated, depended on terrain. The French maquis always aimed to establish 'national redoubts' such as that at Vercours near Grenoble in June 1944, but this was attempting too much and some 3500 maquis were eliminated by two German divisions in pitched battles there. In Yugoslavia, too, large-scale battles were fought but Tito was invariably able to withdraw the bulk of his forces from the seven separate German offensives launched against the partisans between November 1941 and September 1944. In the Soviet Union, of course, initial resistance developed from Soviet troops cut off by the speed of the German advance in 1941 rather than from any spontaneous local resistance to occupation, and the Soviet partisans became an integral part of the Army.

Subversion might also imply insurrection, but this largely failed with disastrous results, as in the case of the rising in the Jewish ghetto in Warsaw in April 1943 and the rising by the Polish Home Army in the same city in August 1944,

Above: A member of Tito's partisans, Yugoslavia 1944.
Top: Members of a partisan detachment from Turopolje-Posava in Croatia, 1944. The partisans received limited military supplies from external sources.
Right: A suspected collaborator is questioned by members of the French Forces of the Interior at Vernon.
Top right: Members of the French maquis cleaning their weapons in a camp located in the Breton woods.
Top far right: A member of the Resistance in Tinchbray after its liberation. Many maquis did not emerge until the Allied invasion was imminent.

which resulted in the deaths of 200,000 Poles when the Soviets chose not to assist their nominal allies. The rising in Prague in May 1945 was also a catastrophe and the rising in Paris as the Allies advanced from the Normandy bridgehead in August 1944 would have been equally bloody had not the German commander deliberately chosen to eschew the use of armor and to refuse to burn the city. Assassination could also bring reprisals such as that perpetrated on Lidice in Czechoslovakia after Czech agents killed Reinhard Heydrich in June 1942. In view of the dangers of direct action, many resistance groups chose simply to act as Intelligence gatherers and to await the imminent arrival of Allied troops before attempting to take up arms openly.

It is difficult to gauge the success of guerrilla activity during World War II. There were undoubtedly some major successes in Intelligence and in evasion. There were also a number of successful sabotage missions, such as the destruction of most of France's tungsten mines, but immense effort could be devoted to destroying an industrial plant only to discover that another was perfectly capable of making good the deficit in production. The fall of French production in 1942-43 by some ten percent has thus been attributed more to French absenteeism than active sabotage. In terms of military activity, large numbers of German troops were probably tied down, such as the 13 divisions retained in Norway throughout the war, although this also owed much to Adolf Hitler's obsession with the possibility of an Allied invasion of the country. In France the Allied Supreme Commander, General Dwight D Eisenhower, credited the French Forces of the Interior with being worth 15 divisions but, although the Germans were unable to prevent the growth of the resistance in France, they most certainly inflicted considerable damage upon it. The most crucial role was that fulfilled prior to the Allied invasion of France in June 1944. There is little doubt that, through resistance activity, the German Army Group G deployed armor against the maquis that should have been made available to Army Group B facing the main Allied armies. Similarly, the advance of the Waffen SS *Das Reich* Division toward

Normandy was slowed by the resistance but at a fearful price, not least the massacre of the villagers at Oradour-sur-Glâne. In Italy an estimated 30,000 partisans operating after Italy's surrender to the Allies succeeded only in executing Benito Mussolini and his mistress. But, as in Spain during the Peninsular War, guerrilla activity was more important in moral and psychological terms and in sustaining hope and restoring national pride.

Most has been claimed for the partisans in the Soviet Union and in Yugoslavia. Many of these claims are wildly exaggerated. In the Soviet Union there was something of a tradition of partisan warfare; the Bolsheviks had deployed partisan units during the Civil War (1917-21) and had also trained guerrilla units during the Spanish Civil War (1936-39). There were, however, no prewar plans to use partisans in defense

of Russia and it was only as a result of the unexpected German invasion that Stalin broadcast on 3 July 1941 to call upon the Soviet people to resist the invaders in a guerrilla war. The partisans, however, were Soviet troops cut off by the German advance and throughout the war they remained closely controlled by the Soviet authorities, the principal command structure being dominated by the NKVD (secret police). Large areas of the Soviet Union were not in fact suited to partisan warfare and guerrilla activity was confined to the forests and marshes of central European Russia – an area which was the responsibility of the German Army Group Center. From a strength of perhaps 30,000 in 1941, the Soviet partisans reached a maximum strength of perhaps 400,000 or 500,000 by the end of 1943, but actual fighting with the Germans was surprisingly limited in view of the numbers involved.

Increasingly, the Soviet partisans were closely woven into the operations of the Red Army and, as the Soviets advanced after 1943, so those partisans in areas now liberated were simply absorbed directly into the army. They were chiefly employed to disrupt German communications, although deep penetration raids were also attempted on occasions. Attacks on German supply lines did have some impact in slowing down troop movements, curtailing supplies reaching the front and destroying vital rolling stock. In the case of the effort mounted in early 1943 to disrupt the main railroad to Bryansk, the partisans appear to have succeeded in postponing 'Operation Citadel,' the planned German offensive. Partisans also laid some 8000 mines on railroads in August 1943 to coincide with the Soviets' own offensive following the battle of Kursk.

They also acted as an arm of Soviet government and collected taxes but they were unable to hinder the German economic exploitation of occupied areas such as the Ukraine, with its valuable agriculture, and the mines and metallurgical industries of the Dnepropetrovsk and Donbas regions.

It is also clear that the Germans devoted relatively few resources to fighting Soviet partisans. Large areas of occupied territory were never garrisoned by the Germans, such as the area around Minsk where partisans were active from 1942 onward, and the German front line was far from continuous. German commanders had learned to operate with highly mobile forces in independent roles and were not overly disturbed by the prospect of partisans operating in their rear. They were content to hold the main roads and railroads, mostly with second-rate troops and the forces of their Hungarian, Rumanian or Italian allies, plus locally raised minorities. Front-line German formations were rarely employed, and then limited to combing forest lairs of the partisans. The Germans invested so few resources in counter-

Left: Representative Yugoslav partisan 'types' taken for propaganda purposes by British photographers. Below: A German armored train protects workmen repairing tracks damaged by Soviet partisans, 1944.

Top left: German troops with captured Soviet partisans, 17 September 1943. Above: M E Kayas, a Soviet partisan who was awarded the Order of the Red Star.

partisan warfare that the considerable effort devoted to partisan operations by the Soviet High Command appears questionable. Where partisans did become of more value was after 1943 when the Germans were on the retreat and German commanders, faced with Hitler's fanatical demands to hold every ditch to the last man, were less free to make tactical withdrawals and more concerned to keep their communications open.

The partisan war in Yugoslavia provides a contrast to that in the Soviet Union. Tito's partisans, for example, did not have the ready recourse to aerial support enjoyed by Soviet partisans; Tito received only moral support from the Soviet Union from 1942 onward and only limited material support from the Allies from April 1943. Resistance had begun following the invasion of Yugoslavia by German and Italian forces in April 1941; Hungary, Rumania and Bulgaria also joined in the partition of the spoils. Uprisings occurred in Croatia in July and in Bosnia and Serbia in August, the movement spreading as the bulk of the German forces were withdrawn for the coming campaign in Russia and with the establishment of quisling regimes such as that of the Ustashas of Ante Pavelić in Croatia. One of the first to resist was Mihailovich, the head of the Yugoslav Army's Operations Bureau attached to the General Staff, who called his followers *Cetniks* after Serbian bands that had fought the Turks in earlier years: Mihailovich appears to have wanted to wait before undertaking military operations, but his hand was forced by the emergence of the communists, led by the 50-year-old general secretary of the Yugoslav Communist Party, Josip Broz (known as Tito). The communists resolved on resistance on 30 June 1941 and their ranks steadily increased from perhaps 15,000 men in 1941 to as many as 200,000 or 300,000 by 1943. The 1st Proletarian Brigade was formed in December 1941, the 2nd in February 1942, the 4th in June 1942 and the 7th in November 1942.

Whereas Mihailovich was a royalist in his sympathies and intended to serve Serbia and the Yugoslav crown, Tito's war was always intended to result in a social and political revolution. Thus

each state within Yugoslavia had its Anti-Fascist Committee of Liberation owing allegiance to the Anti-Fascist People's Liberation Council headed by Tito himself. In areas 'liberated' from the Germans or their allies, the partisans established their own administration and a provisional parliament held its first session at Bihac in Croatia in November 1942. The whole of the command structure was firmly under communist control, so much so that even Stalin reproved Tito for possibly deterring bourgeois patriots from joining the partisans. There were some discussions between Tito and Mihailovich, who was widely recognized in Allied circles (including the Soviet Union) as the authentic voice of Yugoslav resistance, but

nothing came of the attempted union. The two forces drifted into opposition to one another, the Cetniks attacking Uzice in the fall of 1941 and Mihailovich openly co-operating with the Axis powers.

Tito finally won Allied approval in 1943 and the Allies both supplied weapons and regularly evacuated Yugoslav wounded, but to a very great extent Tito liberated his own country without substantial external assistance. In the process, he created the fabric of a new socialist state through political activity hand-in-hand with military action. However, it must be recognized that the Germans afforded relatively little priority to Yugoslavia once the war against the Soviet Union began and it is debat-

Soviet partisans 'defending their village.' In fact, most Soviet partisans were regular troops cut off by the German advance.

able whether, as the partisans claimed, 15 German divisions were tied down in Yugoslavia by the end of the war. The Germans consigned mostly second-rate, over-aged troops to Yugoslavia and local German commanders adopted a 'make do' attitude in a role that was basically a holding action interspersed with occasional forays. The seven main German efforts took place in November 1941 in Serbia, early 1942 in Bosnia, June 1942 in Montenegro, January to April 1943 in Herzegovina, Montenegro and Dalmatia, May to August 1943 in Monte-

negro, the spring of 1944 throughout most of the country, and, lastly, another general offensive in the summer of 1944. Local German administration was a shambles of competing agencies and the Axis was bedevilled by rivalries between the Germans and the Italians, whose troops were largely passive. The Germans were also handicapped by the need to rely upon the Ustashas in Croatia and by their frequent resort to taking hostages as a reprisal, which was not suspended until 1944. Indeed, the war was bitterly fought with no quarter given; for example, the German 1st Mountain Division exceeded its already brutal orders to burn and shoot in the spring offensive of 1943. With so many competing groups it was hard to distinguish friend from foe and as one historian has described it, 'any of these groups might, not necessarily waiting to be provoked, open fire on almost any of the others.' German mortality rates were, however, low and the war was far more characteristically a civil war between the different Yugoslav factions. Most guerrilla success came only after the capitulation of the Italians, Tito swiftly disarming the ten Italian divisions stationed in Yugoslavia. By this time, the partisans had become, as Tito had always intended, very much a conventional army.

In terms of the actual fighting, the guerrilla phase of the war reflected any guerrilla struggle at virtually any time, as indicated by an official report of the German General Wisshaupt, commenting on operations by the 698th Infantry Regiment in Bosnia in January 1942:

The guerrillas were everywhere and nowhere. It was possible to disperse them, but not to destroy them completely. They defended themselves in their positions in the rocks, and then quickly dispersed again into their villages, where they acted like 'peaceful' peasants in a 'friendly' manner toward our troops.

By 1945, therefore, the pattern of guerrilla warfare was well established. It was a form of struggle that could be protracted through the ability of the guerrillas to evade much larger numbers of regular troops committed against them, provided that the terrain was difficult enough to impede the mobility of the

regulars. By contrast with regulars, the guerrillas would usually be lightly equipped and would enjoy greater local knowledge as well as greater mobility. To survive, however, the guerrillas would probably require at least the acquiescence of the local population if not their actual support. In cases where guerrilla war was in any case a response to foreign invasion and occupation, this degree of support would be likely to be automatic. As well as being a resort of the weak, however, it had been increasingly recognized that guerrilla tactics might be employed in conjunction with conventional operations, with guerrillas acting as auxiliaries to regular troops. This mode of guerrilla employment was likely to achieve greater success than isolated guerrilla activity since, in most but not all situations, guerrilla war could not succeed unless there was substantial external assistance or an external refuge from which guerrillas could operate. These basic principles had long been accepted, but without becoming a structured theory of guerrilla war.

Guerrilla warfare, however, was becoming more than merely a tactical method and some theorists and practitioners had already grasped the political implications of guerrilla struggle. The IRA campaign in Ireland is one such example and the political motivation of Communist guerrillas in states such as Yugoslavia and Greece during World War II was another pointer to the future. Some of the most significant developments were those in Southeast Asia, for Japanese occupation undermined the whole basis of European colonial authority and actively fomented nationalism. Those Asian nationalists who had fought against the Japanese, or had fought with them, were fully prepared to continue the struggle against the returning colonial powers if their demands for self-determination and independence were not granted. Thus guerrilla wars were to erupt in Malaya (1948-60), the Philippines (1949-54), the Dutch East Indies (1945-46) and in French Indochina (1946-54). Such nationalists were also able to draw inspiration from yet another practitioner of guerrilla war in whose theories revolutionary politics and guerrilla tactics were to merge inexorably – Mao Tse-tung.

2. SOUTHEAST ASIA
THE IMPACT OF MAO TSE-TUNG

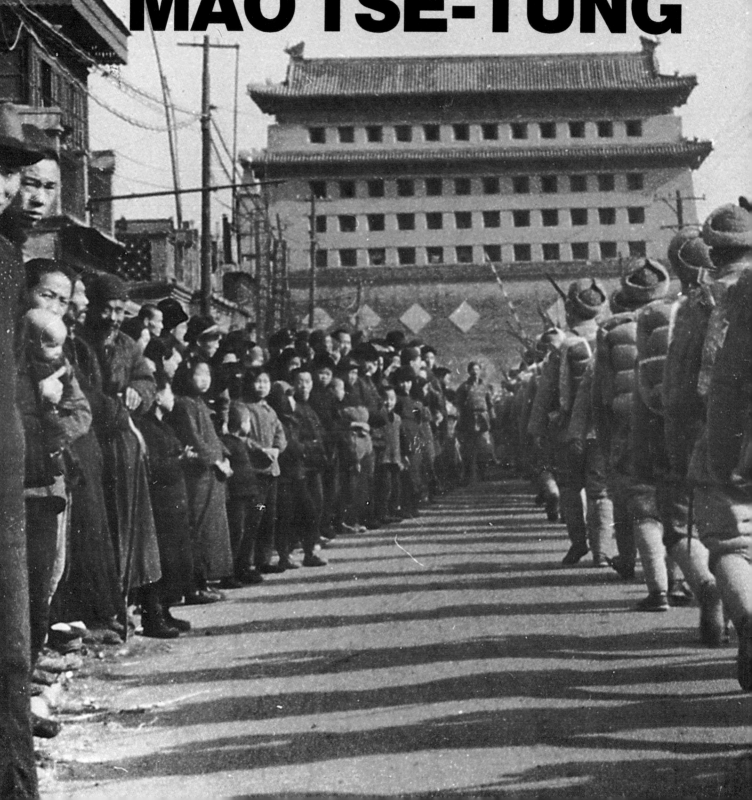

The triumph of the Maoist system of protracted war: regular troops of the People's Liberation Army enter Peking in 1949.

The Maoist system of waging war is a product of the peculiar historical circumstances prevailing in China in the early twentieth century, and of the genius of Mao Tse-tung. Born in 1893, the son of a relatively prosperous Hunan peasant, Mao could never accept the China of his youth, beset with poverty, the rapacious policies of landlords, warlords, corrupt officials and ineffective emperors. The fall of the Manchu dynasty in 1911 only made things worse, throwing much of northern and central China into chaos, and it was out of this chaos that the Chinese Communist Party emerged in 1921. Mao initially occupied a very lowly position in the Party, but after the abortive Autumn Harvest Uprising of 1927, based upon a Russian model of urban revolt that was inapplicable to the rural poverty of China, he began to assume a new importance among the peasants of the Chingkang mountains. Between 1927 and 1949 the Maoist theory of war was dynamic and fluid, constantly evolving to counter new threats and exploit opportunities. It became the most radical, violent and extensive theory of war ever put into effect. Mao devised it from a study of ancient and modern writings on war, modified and supplemented by his acute observations of external events and personal experiences. His seizure of power in Peking in October 1949 proved the applicability of the theory to the reality of revolution and acted as a model for insurgency groups elsewhere, particularly in the similar circumstances of post-1945 Southeast Asia.

Within his general theory of struggle, Mao saw guerrilla warfare as only one element. To him, struggle consisted of a precise compound of psychological, economic, regular military and guerrilla measures. This concept goes far beyond the definition of war given by theorists such as Karl von Clausewitz – the continuation of policy by other means – and aims at nothing less than the total transformation of social and economic structures, not just within China, but throughout the world. An adherent of Clausewitz aims to change the policy of another state; an adherent of Mao wishes to destroy imperialism, feudalism and bureaucratic capitalism. To achieve such aims, the use of force is indispensable – a revolution cannot be peaceful. But the force used must be carefully measured and controlled; an excess of violence can be harmful. It is within this context that guerrilla warfare must be considered, and it is worth bearing in mind throughout that Mao never expected the guerrilla alone to achieve final victory. That could only come when the guerrillas had evolved into regular conventional armies, capable of taking on and defeating the military forces of a central authority weakened and demoralized by guerrilla, economic, political and social pressures.

Mao began to develop his technique of armed struggle in 1927, as the ruling Kuomintang (Nationalist Party) purged itself of all identifiable communists. In response the communists staged a series of uprisings, all of which failed, and it was in the aftermath of these that Mao set up his base in the Chingkang mountains, a wooded wilderness into which the Nationalists rarely ventured. There were some 10,000 communists in the base, of whom about a quarter were armed, and their first move was to attract and absorb the bandits in the region. Having secured their base, they set out to extend their political influence by means of propaganda and terrorism in neighboring villages. They conducted a series of experiments using different forms of organization, but their activities soon attracted the attention of both the Kuomintang and the local warlord. After a blockade of the base, the communists were forced to leave the mountains in 1929, although they had learned some valuable lessons, not least that in order to survive it was essential to have the willing and active support of the mass of the rural population. If the peasants could be recruited, they could provide Intelligence, manpower, food and shelter, creating a buffer between the political leadership of the revolution and the enemy force.

The vital question now was how to recruit such support, and this became a central feature of the Maoist doctrine, producing a closely integrated political and military framework that was to prove both effective and durable. The first stage involved the use of covert agitation to arouse the peasants' anger at

their miserable circumstances and against their local oppressors. The next stage entailed the creation of a Peasant Association in the village. The communist 'work team' of three would choose a committee of poor peasants to screen all members of the village and determine their social class, before calling a meeting just of those who would be likely to be suffering under the current system. Under the guidance of Party members, the meeting would elect an Executive Committee and pass resolutions on policy, attacking the power and social position of landlords, rich peasants and moneylenders. Rents and rates of interest would be arbitrarily reduced, debts cancelled and taxes redistributed. The Peasant Association would take over local judicial functions, confiscate land, disarm the Min Tuan (landlords' militia) and appoint politically reliable poor peasants to be village constables.

Of course, such measures were not accepted peacefully by the rural élite, and Peasant Associations could only be set up and sustained in the presence of Red Army forces, which dealt with any armed resistance by the Min Tuan or other 'reactionary' elements. However, the Red Army troops also gave the peasants confidence in the communists by their own discipline, by political propaganda and by assisting in the work of social reform. Mao believed that the

Above left: A symbol of old China, a mandarin c 1900.
Above: Misery under the Nationalist regime: every winter many poor people died of cold and starvation.
Above right: Mao in 1925.
Right: Mao preaching social revolution to north Chinese peasants during the anti-Japanese War, 1937-45.

role of the army was vital and that the soldiers could only operate effectively in their social tasks if they were subject to very strict standards of personal discipline and behavior. In contrast to the traditional conduct of Chinese soldiers, the Red troops were required to be polite, to pay for all goods taken and to give back everything they borrowed. They took a full part in the political work of convincing the peasants that they could overthrow their masters and at times supplemented exhortation with a selective use of terrorism against class enemies.

If anti-communist forces approached the village, an assessment of their strength would be made. If they were strong, the Red forces would vanish back to their wild sanctuary and the political organs would go underground until the enemy had gone. If it was considered that the enemy could be defeated, the Reds would fight. Every small victory on the field of battle helped the political transformation of the village,

but it was absolutely vital to win, for any small check would have a disproportionately negative effect.

This integration of military and political activity at village level was very delicate and many errors were made in the early stages. Every village infiltrated and taken constituted a different situation which had to be analysed carefully before the first move was made. In general, the policy was to concentrate first on the poorest and most miserable communities, then proceed from them to the less distressed. The process could be a long one; in some villages it took months to

overcome the peasants' fear of the landlords and persuade them to act. Such delays could lead to impatience and forceful action by local Red commanders, but Mao was disposed to proceed gently, by persuasion, convinced that a genuine voluntary spirit would result in better discipline and firmer loyalty than compliance through compulsion.

Although at this time Mao was occupied primarily with issues of civil-military relations, he did begin to interest himself in strategy and tactics. With regard to strategy, he favored concentrating all efforts in a cumulative

Soldiers of the Kuomintang Army enter Shanghai during the Northern Expedition of 1926-28.

infiltration of the countryside. This was contrary to the policy advocated by the Central Committee of the Communist Party, which wanted to seize power by urban uprisings. In the deployment of forces, Mao took account of the activities of the enemy. If no substantial enemy force was in prospect, the Red Army would be dispersed in small detachments supporting political work teams; if an enemy force approached, the detachments would concentrate. A weak enemy would be attacked, most usually by ambush, a strong enemy evaded by a wide circling maneuver. Under pressure, the Red Army would simply scatter and dissolve, some soldiers taking to the hills and others merging into the rural population – a policy very similar to the traditional methods of guerrilla warfare.

Once the communists had been forced out of the Chingkang mountains in 1929, they made their way to South Kiangsi, beyond the sphere of their immediate warlord enemy. They found a new inaccessible fastness and began to establish a new political base. Similar 'soviets' were in preparation in other suitable areas of southern China, but they soon came under attack from the Kuomintang. Between 1930 and 1934 the Nationalist leader, Chiang Kai-shek, ordered five 'Annihilation Campaigns' against the soviets. Only the last was effective, being led by Chiang himself, ably advised by General von Seeckt, former Chief of the German General Staff.

On arrival in South Kiangsi, Mao's policy was to use his existing technique to take over villages, intensify the social revolution in those won over and expand the Red Army. Three types of forces came into being: part-time local guerrillas, full-time guerrillas and regulars. The regulars acted as a strategic reserve in the soviet, although at this time they lacked both equipment and specialized military training. Even so, the first four Annihilation Campaigns were countered by a combination of highly mobile conventional operations, with guerrilla activity in the rear of the enemy. The strategy of the regular Red forces was to avoid being attacked and to abstain from carrying out an attack unless certain of success. By success, Mao meant the complete elimination of the enemy force, achieved by surrounding the enemy with a force ten times its size, although the element of surprise or some key moral advantage could be a substitute for numbers. By whatever means the destruction of the enemy was accomplished, it had to be complete, for the sake of the psychological impact on the enemy. As Mao wrote: 'Injuring all of a man's fingers is not as effective as chopping off one of them, and routing ten enemy divisions is not as effective as annihilating one of them.' If an enemy force could be eliminated without fighting – by surrender or subversion – that was even better. The communists worked hard to win over enemy soldiers. They infiltrated agitators into enemy units and they always allowed surrender on easy terms. These efforts were well-rewarded: in 1931 a brigade of the Army of Feng Yu-hsiang (the Christian warlord) defected en masse and in 1932 a whole Kuomintang army of 20,000 men did the same. These erstwhile enemies brought valuable equipment and useful military skills to the Red Army.

Mao observed the operations in progress and constructed a strategic theory in favor of retreat and counteroffensive. According to his view, during a long

Above: Chiang Kai-shek.
Right: Chou En-lai in the 1930s.
Far right: Mao's favored 'younger
brother,' Lin Piao. He served in the
PLA at all levels of command.
Below: The Long March, 1934-35.

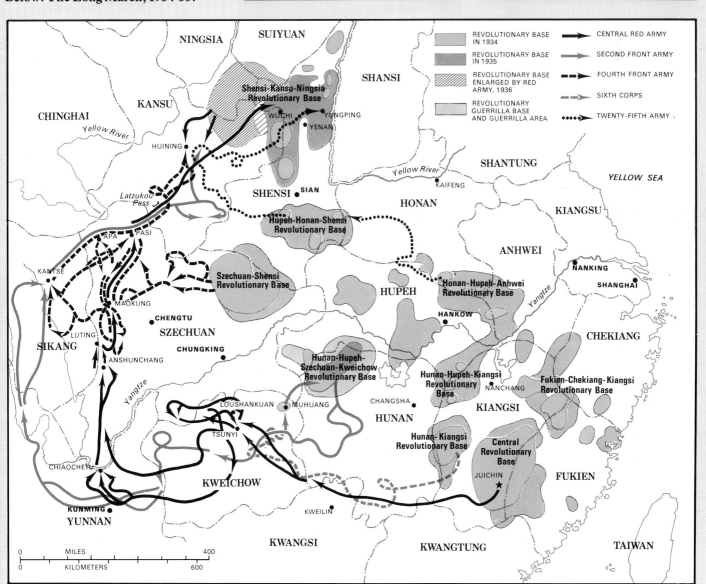

REVOLUTIONARY BASE
IN 1934

REVOLUTIONARY BASE
IN 1935

REVOLUTIONARY BASE
ENLARGED BY RED
ARMY, 1936

REVOLUTIONARY
GUERRILLA BASE
AND GUERRILLA AREA

CENTRAL RED ARMY

SECOND FRONT ARMY

FOURTH FRONT ARMY

SIXTH CORPS

TWENTY-FIFTH ARMY

NINGSIA SUIYUAN SHANSI

KANSU

CHINGHAI

Yellow River

Shensi-Kansu-Ningsia
Revolutionary Base

WUCHI YUNGPING

HUINING YENAN

Latzukou
Pass

SHENSI SIAN

HONAN

Yellow River SHANTUNG

KAIFENG

YELLOW SEA

KIANGSU

APA PASI

Hupeh-Honan-Shensi
Revolutionary Base

ANHWEI

NANKING

SHANGHAI

KANTSE

Szechuan-Shensi
Revolutionary Base

Honan-Hupeh-Anhwei
Revolutionary Base

HUPEH

HANKOW

Yangtze

MAOKUNG

CHENGTU

SZECHUAN

CHEKIANG

LUTING

SIKANG

CHUNGKING

ANSHUNCHANG

Yangtze

Hunan-Hupeh-
Szechuan-Kweichow
Revolutionary Base

Hunan-Hupeh-Kiangsi
Revolutionary
Base

Fukien-Chekiang-Kiangsi
Revolutionary Base

NANCHANG

LOUSHANKUAN

MUHUANG

CHANGSHA

KIANGSI

TSUNYI

HUNAN

CHIAOCHETU

KUNMING

YUNNAN

KWEICHOW

KWEILIN

Hunan-Kiangsi
Revolutionary Base

Central
Revolutionary
Base

JUICHIN

FUKIEN

KWANGSI KWANGTUNG TAIWAN

0 MILES 400

0 KILOMETERS 600

35

retreat the Red forces could watch the enemy closely and identify those units which were weak. These weak units could then be lured by minor provocations, led on through difficult terrain until exhausted and then isolated. Meanwhile, using their superior knowledge of the ground and Intelligence from the population, the Red forces could concentrate sufficient superior forces, in secret, to deliver a crushing blow: a combination of guerrilla and conventional techniques. Mao reckoned that

before the Red forces could risk a general offensive, they had to have created this combination: they must make sure of the active support of the local people; they must enjoy favorable terrain and a local superiority of forces; they must know the exact state of every element of the enemy force; and the enemy must be demoralized and tired.

This strategy was not perfect. One deficiency was that strategic retreats exposed Red villages to the fury of re-

Bottom: A Japanese soldier on sentry duty. The Japanese invasion of 1937 briefly united communists and Kuomintang, but the Japanese could not control all the conquered territory, and behind their lines the covert civil war continued.
Below: Japanese naval Artillery in action in China, 1932. Mao believed that the technical superiority of the Japanese forces would provide only a temporary advantage.

prisals. Mao admitted that it was extremely difficult to explain such maneuvers to a village about to be abandoned. The only means of ameliorating a general loss of confidence was to conduct a vigorous program of hit-and-run attacks on the logistic tail and other 'soft' elements of the enemy army. Another difficulty was that sometimes the enemy refused to disperse his forces in vulnerable detachments. In such cases the Reds could only retreat and wait for the enemy to leave the area of his own free will and in his own time.

The weakness of the Red Army and its mode of warfare was exposed in the 5th Annihilation Campaign in 1933-34. On this occasion the Kuomintang employed good, well-trained troops against the South Kiangsi soviet. They did not attempt to chase the lightly burdened guerrillas, so were not worn out by endless marching. They surrounded the soviet with obstacles, field-works and a road, then divided it into segments by the same means. The fences and blockhouses were held by static infantry, with motorized infantry, artillery and armored cars on call. Aircraft were used for reconnaissance and patrol. The rural population was removed from the vicinity of the barriers and resettled elsewhere. Once the soviet had been securely encircled and cut up, strong mobile columns cleared the segments one by one. Reds who attempted to flee ran up against the barriers and had to fight their way through. Secret police teams dealt with those who attempted to merge into the rural population. All villages were carefully screened and suspects treated ruthlessly. Again and again the Reds had to fight regular troops on an equal basis, and they always lost. As Chiang's net tightened, the communists ran out of room for maneuver and began to get short of food. In October 1934 they were driven to break out and commence the Long March, a grand strategic retreat of some 9500km (6000 miles) to North Shensi. They were pursued and harried all the way, and suffered many casualties. Mao had good reason to reflect upon the folly of proceeding from guerrilla to conventional war too early.

Political and military cadres were left behind in Kiangsi to start the revolutionary process again, but were never able to restore the strength of the original base area. The new base, in North Shensi, was a better natural stronghold, however, and the Kuomintang was soon to be weakened by the actions of the Japanese.

As soon as the communists began to consolidate their new base, Chiang sent his forces to surround them and prepare for a final attack. But his local commanders were reluctant to commit themselves to such an offensive in the face of renewed Japanese aggression from the north. When Chiang arrived at his forward HQ at Sian to take command, his senior subordinates kidnapped him and refused to release him until he had agreed to a United Front with the communists to counter the Japanese. In 1937 the Japanese launched their greatest offensive in China and eventually overran the coastal plain and main river valleys. The Kuomintang forces were pushed back into the southwest; the communists could do nothing to halt the general tide of the enemy advance, although they did win some spectacular local victories, the most important of which was at Pingsing Pass, where a large motorized column was ambushed and destroyed.

Having completed their forward move, the Japanese halted to consolidate. They held all the seaports and most of the major centers of population, and patrolled the railroads and main roads. They were too few to occupy the countryside, so they set up a puppet government and allowed it to raise an army to police rear areas. The communists confined their activities to political moves, with occasional guerrilla raids to sustain their credibility and the morale of the peasants, but in 1940 they launched a major offensive against the Japanese – the '100 Regiments' Campaign. In Phase I, Red Army soldiers and guer-

Far left: The 'Lice on the body of China' – Japanese troops in Manchuria in 1931.
Top: Japanese toast victory when the Kwangtung Army neared the gates of Peking, 1933.
Left: The Kuomintang defends China.

39

rillas, helped by peasants, wrecked the communications network of northern China. Canals were breached, roads dug up, railroad tunnels and tracks blocked or destroyed. In Phase II, isolated Japanese outposts were attacked. This enabled the communists to claim that they were the true leaders of the patriotic national struggle against the invaders, but it provoked a terrible and effective response from the Japanese. In 1941 northern China was subjected to the 'Three-All Campaign,' based on the principles of 'kill all, burn all, destroy all.' Like the Kuomintang in 1934, the Japanese did not attempt to pursue the Red guerrillas; they realized that the whole basis of the Reds' survival was support from the peasantry, so they set out to control the rural population. Villages were occupied, information was gathered by torture and those suspected of communist sympathies were killed or deported. Identity cards were issued and movement strictly controlled; food was seized and issued in rations to prevent any surplus being given to the Reds; and all materials not immediately necessary for life at subsistence level were confiscated. These measures intensified the peasants' hatred of the Japanese, but deprived the Reds of their Intelligence, manpower and material support: there were no further attempts by the communists to mount full-scale attacks on the invaders, although isolated guerrilla raids did continue.

During the course of these events, the communists were constantly learning new lessons and developing their forces. Mao was adding to his own ideas on war and it was during this period that he refined his theory of 'Protracted War.' In his analysis of the long-term prospects, he reached three main conclusions. First, that Japan was only temporarily strong and eventually would prove to be weaker than its enemies, whereas China was potentially much more powerful, being weakened for the moment by political division and poor organization. It followed, as the second conclusion, that the Chinese must wage a long war, so that the weaknesses of the enemy could be exploited and Chinese resources mobilized. Finally, both these processes could be accelerated by guerrilla activity. The Japanese troops in

China, concentrated in cities and on main lines of communication, could be gradually surrounded by hostile countryside and the morale of the Chinese masses slowly improved.

The anti-Japanese war is best seen as a period of preparation for a great war of national liberation that never transpired due to the collapse of Japan in 1945. Mao realized that while guerrilla operations could weaken the Japanese forces they could not defeat them. Large-scale conventional mobile operations would be required to destroy Japanese military units, so it would be necessary to recruit, equip and train regular forces for this task, while at the same time building popular resistance into a powerful and organized movement. Constant guerrilla operations were to be employed not only to weaken the enemy but to train and harden the guerrillas so that they could become regular soldiers, and to obtain arms and supplies by capture. It was also necessary to raise new waves of local guerrillas so that Red villages never felt that local interests had been abandoned in favor of creating centrally controlled forces. In fact, throughout the anti-Japanese war most offensive actions were undertaken, on a small scale, by guerrillas. The seven regular divisions of the Red Army guarded the North Shensi base, with only occasional forays into the hinterland to consolidate ground prepared by the irregulars.

The senior Party organs generally allowed the guerrillas a great amount of tactical freedom. General policy was decided at the highest level, to ensure that regular operations were co-ordinated with guerrilla activity. Actual plans for guerrilla attacks were made and executed at low level, to encourage initiative and flexibility, make full use of local knowledge and ensure that the enemy could never discern a predictable pattern of activity. In this way the Reds maintained a constant succession of small attacks on the enemy, which were of little military effect but great political and ideological value. There were comparatively few direct attacks on the Japanese Army; most actions were against puppet troops, collaborators and Kuomintang loyalists. These enemies were considered 'softer' targets and their elimination had greater long-term politi-

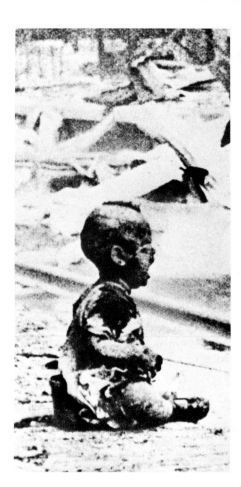

Above: Japanese infantry in Shanghai prepared for chemical warfare.
Top left: An infant in Shanghai after a Japanese bombing raid in 1937.
Left: The results of an air raid on Shanghai, 1937.

cal value. Mao saw the Protracted War not only as the sole means by which China could survive and defeat Japanese aggression but also as a school for the masses. In this brutal school, the masses would learn patriotism, class hatred and self-confidence. They would be driven to confront and understand their situation and prospects, and to adopt self-help under communist guidance. In Mao's own words, '...revolutionary war is an anti-toxin which not only eliminates the enemy's poison, but also purges us of our own filth.'

In 1945 the Japanese were defeated by atomic attack and left China. At once the communists and Kuomintang prepared for a renewal of active civil war. Having analysed the strategic and political situation, the communists acted with speed and vigor. Huge numbers of guerrillas were called up and embodied into

the regular forces. The Red troops were organized into five Field Armies and one of these, the Fourth, was sent to seize southern Manchuria, the industrial heartland of China. Kuomintang forces making their way north to this key area were subject to ambushes and blocking actions, but when they arrived in Manchuria the Reds abandoned the cities and melted into the countryside. The Nationalists were able to occupy and hold the cities, but were never able to control the terrain between and around them. The Reds imposed blockades, then sieges, on city after city. Strong relief forces were evaded, weak ones ambushed and destroyed; agitators inside the cities infiltrated and undermined the garrisons and Kuomintang attempts to resupply by air failed.

As shortages and the threat of starvation increased, so the Kuomintang soldiers became vulnerable to communist propaganda. When the garrison of a city was considered weak enough, and when it could be isolated from relief or reinforcement, the communists made their assault. This generally consisted of an artillery bombardment (using guns

Left: Members of the Canton Women's Defense Corps scaling a wall.

Below left: Chou En-lai (left), the educated and sophisticated diplomat; Chu Teh (right), who became C-in-C of the Red Army; Mao himself (center) reconciled revolutionary politics with military realities.

Below: Soldiers of the Eighth Route Army, the main regular mobile force of the Red Army during the anti-Japanese War, under nominal Kuomintang command from 1936-41, hence the Nationalist flag.

taken from the defeated Japanese and sometimes served by Japanese POWs), followed by concentric massed infantry assault. On occasion, the psychological warfare against the garrison had been so effective that resistance was minimal. Of the Kuomintang soldiers taken prisoner, some 80 percent of other ranks would be enlisted into the Red Army, after a rigorous vetting to exclude class enemies. The loss of these cities had a cumulative and negative effect on the morale of the Kuomintang and helped to shake the solidarity of its senior members. More and more Nationalist units refused to advance, or defected, or dissolved through desertion.

By late 1947 the Reds had commenced continuous regular mobile operations. In battle after battle their superior morale and Intelligence, as well as their mobility, brought them victory. In 1948 the garrison of the Peking-Tientsin pocket, surrounded by the Reds in a series of extensive maneuvers, accepted 'peaceful reorganization' and was incorporated into the People's Liberation Army. The fall of Peking precipitated a progressive collapse of most of the Kuomintang formations to the south. In October 1949 the People's Republic of China was proclaimed.

During this period of civil war Mao did not produce any startling new theories, but he did reaffirm and codify existing principles and techniques. He continued to insist that all guerrilla and conventional-force action should be prosecuted to destroy enemy units and not just to occupy ground. He repeated that superior morale and the support of the people were the only reliable means of ensuring victory, and that these factors could only be guaranteed by strong discipline, based upon political education and the principle of unity: '...Army and people united, army and government united, officers and soldiers united, and the whole country united.' Unity with the people was guaranteed by the prosecution of a just revolutionary war and enforcement of established standards of behavior towards the peasantry. Unity of army and government was achieved by the machinery of political dual control and implementa-

Left: A local guerrilla soldier prepares to execute a class-enemy, probably an unpopular landlord or moneylender. Below left: Chiang and Madame Chiang riding with Lord Louis Mountbatten, Allied Supreme Commander in Southeast Asia. Below: A communist machine-gun team in action, equipped with a Japanese weapon. 'Let the enemy be your quartermaster' was one of Mao's principles.

tion of 'Three Check-ups,' all soldiers being assessed on the basis of class origin, performance of duty and enthusiasm in battle. The relations between officers and men were governed by a system of military democracy: soldiers were required to engage in criticism of themselves, each other and their officers, so as to identify and resolve potential grievances before they became disruptive.

To improve performance in battle, Mao produced a set of '10 Commandments' on tactics. These represented a codification of the usual tactical procedures of the Red forces. They were to select isolated and scattered enemy units for their first attacks and then to deal with stronger concentrations. They were to take the rural areas and small towns first, then besiege the cities. The constant aim was to destroy complete enemy units, never to push back an enemy force or to take or hold ground. To win a formal battle, they must achieve a superiority of forces, encircle the enemy, attack suddenly from all directions at once and avoid the development of a battle of attrition. Attacks were to be prepared very carefully, especially with regard to the collection of Intelligence and psychological preparation of the assault troops, and only launched if certain to succeed. The soldiers were to be encouraged to heroic self-sacrifice by exhortation and example and must be prepared to make successive attacks without rest, if opportunities were apparent. If possible the enemy forces were to be attacked on the move; enemy commanders were to be made to feel insecure by demonstrable threats to strongpoints, bases, lines of retreat and supply routes. Great cities were to be taken with maximum publicity, once they were obviously weak. The enemy was to be the main source of recruits, weapons and the material of war. In temporary lulls, the troops were to be allowed to rest, but given intensive political instructions; the enemy was never to be allowed to rest.

To sum up the Maoist theory of guerrilla war from within all this, it is possible to make certain generalizations and state some rules which withstood a series of rigorous practical tests. The first general principle is that, in all questions, political and ideological factors must be supreme. No military advantage can ever compensate for a loss of political direction. The second is that a guerrilla force can survive and operate only with the active support of the mass of the population, so political preparation of the masses, sustained by the reassuring presence of perfectly behaved and apparently strong armed forces, must come before any military activity. The third is that human factors are more decisive than material factors, in every stage or form of conflict. Morale not weapons wins battles and wars. Once active, guerrillas must be subject to firm central guidance on policy and strategy, but must have local control of tactics: there must be 'Strategic Centralization, Tactical Devolution.' Guerrillas must never be allowed to remain mere irregulars but must constantly be improved by training and experience and organized into larger formations, until they can fight as regulars. Against a regular enemy force, only conventional operations can be fully effective in the end. Once operations are commenced, all forms of defensive action are to be avoided. Only attacks certain to succeed and sure to wipe out whole enemy units or formations are of any value. The enemy forces are to be weakened and, if possible, destroyed by psychological measures rather than by fighting. If fighting is inevitable, attacks are to be made in such a way as to maximize surprise, by ambush or after a covert approach to an enemy in position. A formal attack must always be made with at least ten to one numerical superiority if the enemy is unshaken. All enemy forces are to be attacked at their weak points, split up and eliminated piecemeal if possible. If the enemy is locally or temporarily strong, the guerrillas are to evade his forces by maneuver, by taking refuge in the nearest sanctuary or by blending into the local population. The whole army of guerrillas is to be founded on the 'base unit' of the company, about 120 strong, controlled by a commander and a political officer. The company is to be the focus of loyalty and all activity for the soldier. All actions at battalion level or above are simply agglomerations of company actions.

According to the Maoist theory, a national war of liberation takes place in three phases. In Phase I, the preparatory phase, political work teams identify the

Below: PLA regulars receive familiarization training on the US-manufactured Thompson submachine gun, a weapon particularly useful for small-scale ambushes.

Above: In pursuit of the Kuomintang. After the collapse of the nationalists in the Peking-Tientsin pocket, the PLA regulars crossed the Yangtze River in 1949, the last great strategic barrier.

most discontented elements of the masses, those with intractable grievances and no hope of redress. These people must be persuaded by agitators to believe that by their own actions they can improve their lot. They must be formed into cells and trained as cadres. By provoking repressive measures on the part of the enemy, more of the poor will be inspired to take up arms against authority. Propaganda, disorder and terrorism are to be used to wreck the local structure of government and paralyse the traditional élite. The shift of power is to be consolidated by a redistribution of material assets so that tentative revolutionaries have a direct interest in maintaining the revolution.

In Phase II, once a large-enough base area has been created in Phase I, there are to be active operations against enemy forces, to extend the base area into the 'contested zone,' where both guerrillas and their enemy can operate. The aim of these operations is to extend the base area at the expense of the contested area, eroding the enemy base area by contesting it, segment by segment. A contested area becomes a base area when the guerrillas can appear in it by daylight. In the contested area the guerrillas are able to move freely at night, but usually lie up in daytime. As always, political indoctrination and military operations are to go hand in hand. Terrorism, sabotage and minor forms of attack (ambushes, raids,

the use of booby-traps) are to be employed, mainly behind enemy lines. Enemy pushes or sweeps are to be treated in accordance with Mao's simple and well-known formula:

The Enemy advances; we retreat;
The Enemy halts; we harass him;
The Enemy evades action; we attack;
The Enemy retreats; we pursue.

In Phase III, having weakened the enemy and built up adequate forces and base areas, the revolutionaries are to conduct regular operations of war to invade the enemy base area and eliminate his forces. At that stage the revolutionaries will be in a position to take over power in the state and to put into effect

their political and social reforms. Of course, the transition from Phase II to Phase III requires very careful timing if it is not to be premature. Maoists believe that if a premature shift to Phase III leads to military catastrophe, it is possible to revert to Phase II or even Phase I, and to repeat a portion of the cycle. This may well place an intolerable strain on the patience of the peasantry, however, for whom the war is supposedly being fought.

The end result of all this is the usurpation of political power and it is in this respect that Mao differed so much from the theorists and practitioners of traditional guerrilla war. They had seen guerrillas as representative of military desperation – when a regular army had been defeated or was not available, then elements of the local population, desperate to fight the rule of an oppressive or alien ruler, would use the skills at their disposal to wear the enemy forces down preparatory to the reappearance of a regular army – and had never expected the small bands of partisans to achieve victory on their own. What Mao did was to take these principles and mold them into a revolutionary process, tying them to the political and ideological framework of a set of firm beliefs designed to replace those of the existing rulers of a state. Within this process, the guerrillas had an integral part to play, protecting the 'safe bases' of the revolution from attack and gradually wearing down the conventional armed forces of the ruling authorities. The aim was to cause such armed forces to stretch themselves thinly in protection of cities, towns and lines of communication, for this would leave them vulnerable not only to continued guerrilla pressure but also to more conventional attack by the regular units of the revolution. Once under pressure, they would find it difficult to respond, being under attack at both guerrilla and conventional levels, and would quickly become demoralized. Their defeat in open battle would leave the central body of state government exposed and enable the revolutionaries to assume the reins of office. It was a complex process, dependent upon a number of intangible factors and an enormous amount of political as well as military effort, but it did provide a new role for the guerrilla and, once Mao had succeeded in China, an apparent 'model' for campaigns elsewhere.

In fact, Mao believed that his basic principles of struggle could be applied to all levels of conflict in all parts of the world. At the world level he applied his doctrine by supporting 'wars of national liberation' in the Third World. In the 1960s, as decolonization began to accelerate, he drew an analogy between the state of the world and Manchuria in the Chinese Civil War. According to him the developed industrial countries of the world corresponded to the cities, garrisoned by the Kuomintang and dependent for their survival on the ruthless and unjust exploitation of the surrounding

countryside. The Third World countries, primary producers of food and raw materials, resembled the countryside and could, led by socialist and anti-imperialist guerrillas, blockade and bring down the developed countries. The guerrillas could not be defeated by the chosen weapons of the developed powers, nuclear missiles. The guerrillas were bound to succeed in the long run, imposing a new world order founded on international social justice. It seemed a convincing and attractive case, particularly to those nationalists in many Third World states who were fighting for their freedom against imperial powers or the apparently pro-imperialist governments left behind after decolonization.

Attempts to export the Maoist system, however, have had mixed results. On the whole it appears to work only in areas under predominantly Chinese cultural influence. A version of the Maoist form worked in Vietnam, traditionally regarded as a southern extension of the Chinese empire. In Malaya, adverse circumstances and resolute action by the ruling authorities combined to defeat the guerrillas. It is instructive to compare the two examples.

The Vietnamese Communist Party, founded in 1930 by the Annamese revolutionary Ho Chi Minh, took advantage of World War II to build up political and military organizations and to represent itself as a patriotic resistance movement,

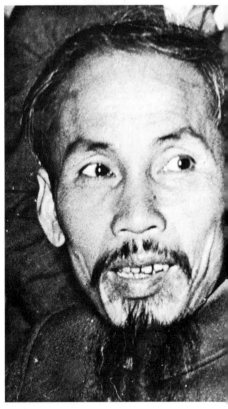

Top: The spirit of insurrection lives on. A rally in Shensi during the Great Proletarian Cultural Revolution.
Above: The successful disciple of Mao, Ho Chi Minh, leader of the Vietnamese Communists.
Top right: Chiang Kai-shek observes his army in training, Taiwan, 1950s.
Right: General Giap addresses a local Viet Minh guerrilla unit in 1944.

initially against the Vichy French colonial rulers and then against the Japanese. By 1945 the Communist Party was the dominant political movement in Vietnam, and although its strength tended to be concentrated in the north, around Hanoi and Haiphong, it was poised to take full advantage of the collapse of Japan. When this occurred in August, the Viet Minh (as the communists were known) took control of northern Vietnam and, with help from the American Office of Strategic Services (OSS), frustrated initial attempts by the French to reassert their former colonial control. This gave the communists political credibility among the peasants and enabled them to build up a strong measure of popular support – a vital prerequisite of the Maoist model. Even when the victorious Allies insisted on sending troops into Indochina (Vietnam, Laos and Cambodia), ostensibly to disarm and repatriate the surrendered Japanese, Ho Chi Minh's government in Hanoi survived, experiencing no effective opposition from the Nationalist Chinese forces which occupied Vietnam down to the 16th Parallel. Further south, however, British forces made the return of the French authorities much easier and the communists were confined to political actions along the lines of Mao's Phase I. Nevertheless, the French were never able to re-establish full authority over the country. The Viet Minh opposed them by political agitation, demonstrations and guerrilla attacks. The French were never able to deploy enough troops to garrison the towns, secure the main roads between them and conduct a proper campaign of counterinsurgency, particularly when, in March 1946, they managed to replace the Nationalist Chinese in the north, for this extended their area of responsibility at a time when the number of French troops in Indochina was declining.

In October 1949 the communist victory in China gave the Viet Minh, by this

**Right: French paras at Dien Bien Phu.
Top right: Communist troops at Dien Bien Phu were resupplied by bicycle.
Far right: Viet Minh move into a village set on fire by the retreating French. The ex-guerrillas are transformed into regular soldiers.**

time firmly established in 'safe bases' in northeastern Vietnam (the Viet Bac), an important new advantage, for they now had an absolute sanctuary in the Chinese People's Republic and a reliable source of supply for war materials. The French were unable to influence Chinese communist policy and could not deploy enough troops to close the long and inhospitable border. Instead they tried to garrison the rural areas of the north, stationing small detachments in isolated posts in the vain hope that they would be able to police the region. Such a policy played right into the hands of the Viet Minh guerrillas and in 1950, in the aptly named 'War of the Posts,' these garrisons were overwhelmed and destroyed by locally superior communist forces. The process culminated in September 1950 when a Viet Minh attack took out the more substantial garrison of Dong Khe on the northeastern Cao Bang-Lang Son ridge, forcing the French to evacuate their forces to Hanoi. Harried all the way, they lost an estimated 6000 personnel.

This suggested to the communists, and especially to their military leader, Vo Nguyen Giap, that the time was ripe to enter Phase III of the Maoist model, and in 1951 he organized three separate conventional attacks – at Vinh Yen (13-17 January), Mao Khe (23-28 March) and Phat Diem (29 May-18 June) – against the French bases around Hanoi and Haiphong on the Red River delta. This was an error, the consequence either of optimism or impatience. The Viet Minh were not as accomplished as the French at regular warfare and could not make headway against the full weight of modern firepower and air attacks. The offensive failed, at an estimated cost of nearly 12,000 communist lives.

To the French this constituted a major victory, but they were unaware of the inherent flexibility of Maoist warfare. Giap, realizing that the 'revolutionary moment' had not yet arrived, merely reverted to Phase II, deploying his guerrillas to tie down the French while gradually building up regular units preparatory to a renewed offensive on more favorable terms. The process was successful, forcing the French to remain behind fixed defenses (the De Lattre Line) in the Red River delta or in heavily fortified outposts throughout the northern provinces. In general terms, the French maintained a tenuous hold on the urban areas and could move, in protected convoys, between them, but the constant slow attrition in ambushes and skirmishes with the Viet Minh had an adverse effect on morale and, significantly, on public opinion in France. By 1953 the French had been considerably weakened and the time seemed ripe for a more decisive move into Phase III.

The opportunity arose in late 1953 when the French, intent upon drawing the Viet Minh into a battle where the advantages of European firepower could be brought to bear, committed airborne troops to take and hold the valley of Dien Bien Phu, in the northwest of Vietnam astride communist supply lines to Laos. By laborious secret movement, the communists were able to concentrate a large conventional force, complete with artillery and antiaircraft guns, in the hills surrounding the French base. Blocking forces were put into position on all possible resupply or relief routes, forcing the French to depend solely upon air power to sustain their efforts, and a siege commenced. Outlying French positions were overwhelmed and the airstrip at Dien Bien Phu brought under artillery fire, leaving the defenders dependent upon aerial supply drops which did not always arrive (the French were to lose 62 aircraft over the valley before the end of the battle). In early April 1954 Giap enclosed the garrison in a tight ring of fortified trenches and by 7 May, after a siege lasting 55 days, the French were exhausted. Almost 11,000 men surrendered to the communists, representing a defeat from which the French could not recover. With public opinion by now widely opposed to the war, the French government decided to withdraw from their Far Eastern empire.

By the Geneva Agreement of July 1954, Vietnam was divided. In the North, beyond the 17th Parallel, the communists under Ho Chi Minh set up a socialist republic. In the South, the Emperor Bao Dai presided over a government with a democratic form, but was soon thrust aside by Ngo Dinh Diem, a strong political operator with

Inset: Nguyen Xuan Thuy reports back on the Vienna Conference in 1953. International efforts to end the war in Vietnam failed but the communists used them to mobilize foreign support.

Main photo: Helicopter evacuation of French wounded from Dien Bien Phu 1954. The French had few helicopters available, confining their army to ground movement.

powerful friends in the United States. Both Laos and Cambodia became independent states. The South Vietnamese authorities were never able to establish full control over their territory, or to set up an effective machinery of government or to inspire trust and goodwill from their subjects. From its very inception, South Vietnam was plagued by corruption in all the organs of state and by subversive activity. Only increasing US support sustained the Saigon government.

The communists began a program of infiltration and organization of the South Vietnamese countryside in 1955. Their task of politicizing the peasantry was eased by the corrupt, repressive and economically incompetent character of Diem's government. They were also assisted by deep social divisions between the Buddhists and Catholics and between the peasants and the urban population. Active insurgency commenced in 1959, with invulnerable base areas in remote parts of the Central Highlands and complete sanctuary across the Demilitarized Zone (DMZ) on the 17th

Inset, top: Sharpened bamboo poles protect an American artillery position. Inset, bottom: A 'Magpie's Nest' or 'Venus Fly-Trap.' Both the Americans and Viet Cong made use of booby-traps. Below: Flamethrower in action. An American soldier uses this dramatic and controversial weapon, particularly effective in dealing with guerrillas concealed in tunnels or bunkers.

Parallel. Initially the main aim was to destroy the structure of local government by killing officials, headmen and tax collectors. Police and troops sent to protect these victims also became targets, if deemed vulnerable enough. Villagers could not or would not help the government to catch the guerrillas; some had been indoctrinated, others intimidated. In any case the Army of the Republic of (South) Vietnam (ARVN) gave no impression of strength, efficiency or positive motivation. Before long whole areas of the countryside were outside the government's control. The guerrillas, following the Maoist pattern, organized themselves into larger groups and became bolder in their operations. In the northern provinces of South Vietnam, North Vietnamese regulars sometimes led major attacks.

These developments led to a political crisis in Saigon and Diem appealed to the USA for aid, which was promptly given. The American policy appears to have been determined by a simple aversion to communist expansionism, with no deep interest in the character or prospects of Diem's regime in the South. At first, US involvement was material and advisory, with teams of specialists attempting to re-equip and retrain the ARVN and Field Police. However it soon appeared that this was not enough. The communists continued to expand their base areas and areas of active operations. A change of government in Saigon, with the fall of Diem to a military coup in November 1963, did nothing to improve political stability or the efficiency of the ARVN.

In 1965 the US adopted a more forward and vigorous policy. Combat troops of the US Army and Marines were sent to South Vietnam and US aircraft started to bomb the North. From this year onward, the war became a conflict between the US and North Vietnam, with the South Vietnamese as junior partners to the USA. The Americans enjoyed great material and economic advantages and relied on modern technology, firepower and air mobility to win. The North Vietnamese had all the political and psychological advantages. They relied on rigorous social discipline and the will to endure the privations of war indefinitely. The government in

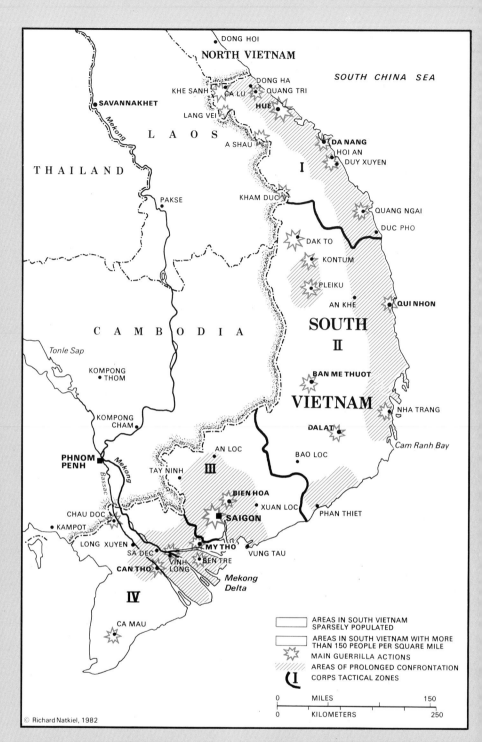

© Richard Natkiel, 1982

AREAS IN SOUTH VIETNAM SPARSELY POPULATED

AREAS IN SOUTH VIETNAM WITH MORE THAN 150 PEOPLE PER SQUARE MILE

MAIN GUERRILLA ACTIONS

AREAS OF PROLONGED CONFRONTATION

CORPS TACTICAL ZONES

Above: Map of South Vietnam at the time of the Tet Offensive.
Top right: A suspected Viet Cong woman is questioned by a member of the Republic of Vietnam's Field Police.

Right: 'Every one a soldier, every soldier a producer.' As in China, the rural masses in North Vietnam were mobilized and controlled by a militia system.

Hanoi was particularly adept at propaganda and exploited the American impatience for a clear and positive conclusion to the war.

The US forces in Vietnam did prevent the North Vietnamese from taking control of South Vietnam and they also recorded many positive achievements, but they never threatened the long-term existence of the Viet Cong (Vietnamese communists) or their masters in Hanoi. There were never enough US combat troops to dominate all significant areas. Attempts to dominate or deny terrain by artillery, bombing and chemical warfare never succeeded and were indiscriminate. This added to the pressure from domestic opinion in the USA. Attempts to liaise and work closely with the ARVN foundered, with mutual misunderstandings, the consequences of cultural dissonance. The US command did not comprehend the Vietnamese people or the nature of the sort of war the enemy was fighting. A blind faith in engineering and investment, as though war were a matter of technological ingenuity and business administration, prevented the necessary hard work of Intelligence gathering and assessment.

The US forces cleared a number of important valleys of Viet Cong forces in 1966-67 by large-scale search-and-destroy operations, followed up by constant intensive patrolling, but they lacked sufficient infantry to exercise permanent control of these areas, especially at night, and the communists simply reverted to Phase I of the Maoist scheme. Intelligence was never good enough to eradicate all communist sympathizers from these areas. The Americans infiltrated the Central Highlands, mainly with Special Forces, and turned a communist sanctuary into a contested zone. They also attempted to disrupt the Viet Cong logistic system by building artillery fire bases to dominate important border crossing points and routes from the DMZ or down the Ho Chi Minh Trail. These operations undoubtedly imposed loss and inconvenience on the communists. On occasion the Viet Minh, with North Vietnamese help, did attempt to isolate and capture fire bases, as at Khe Sanh in early 1968, but found that American strength in helicopters prevented a

Top: US Marines arrest suspected Viet Cong.

Above: To deprive the Viet Cong of their bases people from inaccessible or suspected villages were evicted.

Right: Suspect under interrogation in the field. US forces had little success in gathering useful Intelligence.

repetition of Dien Bien Phu. US attempts to reform the ARVN and re-organize the South Vietnamese civil administration had very limited success, and allowed the Viet Cong to claim that they were fighting a patriotic war against alien imperialists, interfering in the internal affairs of Vietnam. Generally, the communist guerrillas made few serious attacks on US forces (that was left to the North Vietnamese regulars), preferring softer options such as attacks on civil officials, police or selected elements of the ARVN. Most attacks on US forces were made by indirect means, using booby-traps, mines, long-range sniping and rocket attacks from thick cover.

By 1968 it appeared that the war had become a bloody stalemate and, from a purely military viewpoint, could go on for ever. The communists could not wipe out the US forces; the US forces could not find the communists. The bombing of the North (Operation Rolling Thunder) inflicted damage but also did political damage to the USA, and North Vietnam was able to replace much of the loss from Chinese and Soviet sources. But it was in early 1968 that the communists launched their decisive stroke – the Tet Offensive. This consisted of an extensive rural insurrection co-ordinated with attempts to seize and hold a number of important urban centers by conventional means. The communists were repressed and re-pulsed with great loss, but did hold a number of towns, most notably Hué, for some time, forcing the Americans to fight bitter campaigns to reassert their control over what, in the end, were little more than piles of rubble. What mattered was not the military result of the offensive, however, but its impact on American public opinion. The scale and vigor of the communist attack, coming at a time when US commanders were telling President Lyndon B Johnson that victory was in sight, convinced the public that the war in Vietnam could not be won at acceptable cost in reasonable time. There were massive and disorderly demonstrations against US involvement and, amid vociferous political opposition at home and abroad, Johnson halted the bombing of the North in exchange for Hanoi's agreement to talk peace.

The US subsequently embarked on a policy of gradual disengagement, disguised as 'Vietnamization.' The removal of ground forces was accompanied by an intensification of efforts against the supply route down the Ho Chi Minh Trail (in 1970 ARVN forces, backed by US air power, drove deep into both Laos and Cambodia in an effort to close the route), but success was short-lived. President Richard M Nixon and his adviser Henry Kissinger were anxious to 'normalize' relations with China and continued entanglement in Vietnam obstructed the advancement of this policy. But they were also anxious to get out of the war without a great loss of prestige, hence their efforts to upgrade the ARVN so that it could fight alone with only US diplomatic aid and air commitment in the event of a crisis.

The new policy of Vietnamization was apparently working well as the ARVN, backed by renewed US bombing of the North (Operation Linebacker), contained the communist invasion of the South in 1972, but once the US ground forces left Vietnam the nature of the war changed. Despite the agreement of January 1973 which marked the end of overt US involvement, the North did not cease their efforts, striving to achieve the position of military superiority that would enable them to reunite Vietnam under their control. In this they were helped by a number of factors. The trauma of defeat caused many Americans to question the efficacy of continuing to support the South and this was manifested in a gradual cut-back of financial and material aid to Saigon. At the same time, South Vietnamese society remained divided and the government was as chaotic and corrupt as ever. The morale and combat efficiency of the ARVN declined dramatically. When the North Vietnamese Army invaded the South again in March/April 1975, helped by a rising of the Viet Cong, there was little that the Saigon authorities could do. Promised US air support did not materialize, leaving the ARVN isolated and vulnerable. The North Vietnamese communists had finally managed to achieve Phase III of the Maoist pattern after some 34 years of conflict: on 30 April 1975 they entered Saigon, implying that the theories of

Right: The Battle of Hanoi. General Giap congratulates members of a SAM battery near the capital at the height of the American bombing raids.
Bottom: The Viet Cong's lifeline, the Ho Chi Minh Trail.
Below: A Vietnamese soldier, wounded during the 1973 peace talks.

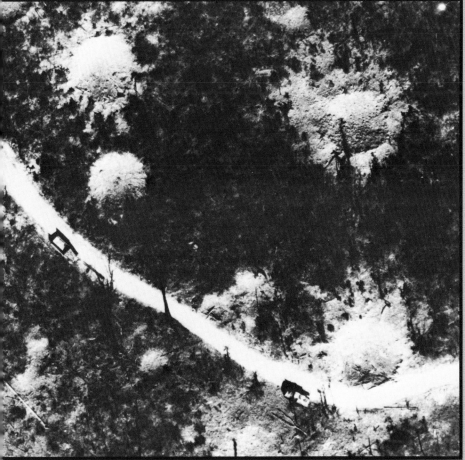

Mao, adapted to fit local conditions, could be successfully applied elsewhere.

This victory must be put into context, however, for although Ho Chi Minh and his followers clearly looked to Mao for inspiration and basic principles, their success was not guaranteed, as may be seen from the example of Malaya between 1948 and 1960. The Malayan communist leader Chin Peng certainly tried to follow the Maoist pattern, setting up safe base areas among the Chinese squatters on the jungle fringes and organizing guerrilla bands which concentrated their attacks on civilian and military targets in an attempt to undermine the British hold on the state. The aim was independence on communist terms. The demand for an end to British rule was attractive to certain elements of Malayan society, but the revolution failed to materialize. The reasons are many and varied – in Malaya the political, economic, geographical and human factors were less favorable to communist revolution than in China or Vietnam – but credit must be given to the British authorities for recognizing and exploiting key advantages.

Above: US troops in action against the North Vietnamese Army.

Below: A Viet Cong with his US captors and his weapon – the much-favored AK-47, supplied by China.

Right: Southeast Asia post-1945.
Below right: British and Malayan troops on jungle patrol, Malaya, 1950s.

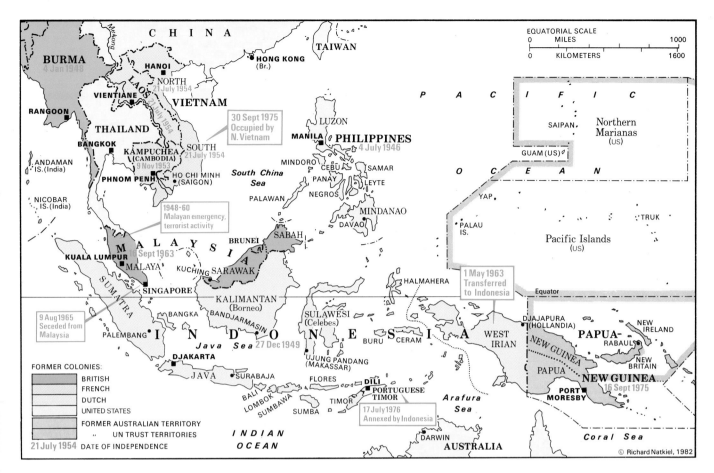

On the political level, the Malayan Communist Party (MCP) was handicapped by interference from Moscow and by its own lack of judgment. In 1948, hard-pressed in Europe, the Soviet Union called on the MCP to lead an anti-British rising. The resultant uprising was premature. The communists revealed themselves before they had made adequate preparations (despite having spent World War II in organization and training as an anti-Japanese partisan force), failed to obtain adequate popular support and were forced to flee into the jungle. They renewed active operations in 1951, but mistook a general desire for independence among the people for a desire for social revolution. Malaya was relatively prosperous, with little real hardship, so there was no impetus for revolution. The British deprived the MCP of nationalist support by giving a credible promise of independence and by making obvious preparations to grant it. So the MCP had no political grounds on which to appeal to the population as a whole.

Geography was also against the MCP. The terrain of Malaya did not favor them. They could find safety in deep jungle but if confined to those areas could not hope to influence the rural population. Unlike the Vietnamese communists, they could not take refuge in China or any neighboring communist state and could not expect massive logistic support from external sources. The MCP also suffered from the population structure of Malaya. The Party itself was largely Chinese, but only a third of the Malayan population was Chinese, the others being Malay and Indian in ethnic origin. Of the Chinese population, moreover, the only element which was potentially available to the MCP was the large number of squatters who lived in unregistered settlements on the jungle fringes. The British dealt with this threat by changing the policy on naturalization to give the squatters a secure place in society, and by land reform to give them a stake in the country. Many were moved into specially built protected villages, away from the jungle and guerrilla activity, so denying the MCP recruits, Intelligence and food.

There were also direct military measures against the guerrillas, to keep

them away from populated areas and to harass them in their sanctuaries. Most offensive operations were based on a careful analysis of Intelligence. Joint committees ensured that all police and military forces pooled their information and acted in concert. Much money was spent to recruit and service informers and infiltrators, and a considerable number of the MCP turned mercenary for the British. The troops in Malaya were primarily infantry. They were given special training to ensure that they treated the civilian population with courtesy and kindness. They received intensive training in minor tactics and night operations. In the field, all was

sacrificed to mobility on foot. The most common operation was the long-range, small, offensive jungle patrol and although contacts with the enemy were rare, they were sufficient to inhibit the guerrillas from moving freely in their chosen base areas.

The result of all this was that the MCP never presented a serious challenge to the authority of the British colonial government or to the plan for independence. By 1953 guerrilla actions were on the decline and thereafter, as attrition and demoralization took hold, they faded away. The guerrillas were not wiped out; they still survive today, but they have been driven to live in the

Far left: Chin Peng, leader of the
Malayan Communist Party.
Left: General Sir Gerald Templer.
Top left: Protected villages in Malaya
housed squatters away from the
guerrilla sanctuaries.

Above: A Malayan police patrol
searches a suspected guerrilla, 1950s.
Below: Resettlement villages were
carefully controlled to deprive
guerrillas of access to food.

remotest parts of the country where they
can have no real influence upon its
future.

To conclude, it would appear from the
examples of Vietnam and Malaya that
the Maoist pattern of revolutionary
warfare, within which guerrilla tactics
play an integral part, is by no means
universally applicable, reflecting the
peculiar conditions and needs of the
China of four decades ago. But this does
not alter the fact that the pattern affected
the way in which people, particularly in
the area of Southeast Asia, have responded to the challenges of nationalism. Mao gave them inspiration, and
although his success in China could not
be duplicated except in the very similar
conditions of Indochina/Vietnam, it was
enough to alter the role of the guerrilla in
the history of warfare. To discover if this
was reflected elsewhere in the emerging
Third World, we need to turn to the
equally violent continent of Africa
during the turbulent years of
decolonization.

Members of a French patrol seek information from the inhabitants of a village in the Algerian interior, May 1956.

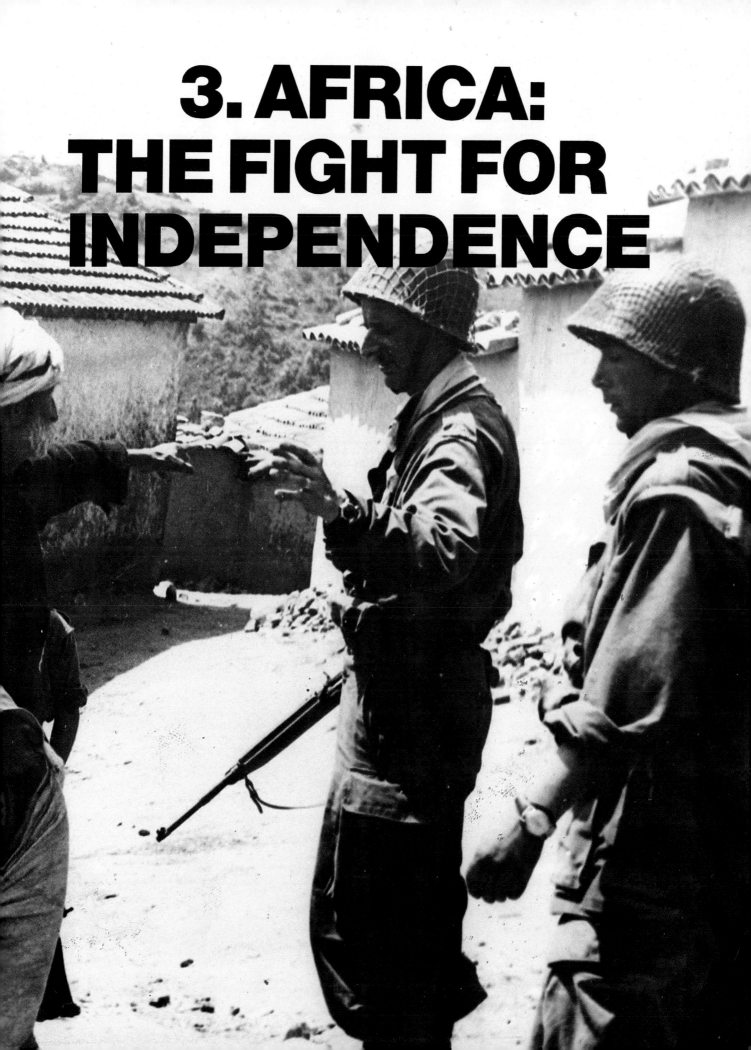

3. AFRICA: THE FIGHT FOR INDEPENDENCE

In 1945 virtually the entire continent of Africa was a colonialist preserve. There were only four independent African states, three of which – Egypt, Ethiopia and Liberia – were still subject to considerable external influence, while a fourth – South Africa – was ruled by an established white minority. The rest of the continent was governed by five imperial powers, Britain, France, Belgium, Portugal and Spain, with the British and the French pre-eminent. These powers were of the opinion that their African subjects would be neither capable nor even desirous of achieving self-government for many years to come.

Such views soon came under challenge. By the late 1940s and early 1950s a new generation of African nationalists was already active. These nationalist leaders, invariably drawn from the Western-educated elites and inspired by Western concepts like national self-determination, were calling for African self-rule, a demand epitomized by the slogan 'Africa for the Africans.' Before very long this demand was realized. As the political, moral, economic and military costs of maintaining an empire rose, the imperial powers were persuaded or coerced into granting independence to their African subjects. This process of decolonization began in the predominantly Arab north of the continent in the early 1950s, affected West Africa in the late 1950s and other parts of Africa during the early and mid-1960s. By 1980 there were 50 independent African states and decolonization had virtually run its course. The only parts of the continent still under external jurisdiction were the tiny Spanish enclaves of Ceuta and Melilla, along the Moroccan coastline, while only in two African territories – South Africa and Southwest Africa (Namibia) – had African nationalism not yet triumphed.

By and large, this transfer of power from European to African was brought about by persuasion rather than coercion. Certainly in most African countries the nationalists achieved their goal without having to use force on a serious and sustained basis. However, there were several notable exceptions to this rule, and in each case the nationalists resorted to the weapon of the weak

against the strong: guerrilla warfare. It took eight years of bloody and vicious conflict to make the French quit Algeria, and even longer to push Portugal out of Guinea-Bissau, Angola and Mozambique. The British too faced a serious guerrilla revolt in one of their African colonies, Kenya. African nationalists also resorted to force in order to overthrow white supremacy in Rhodesia (Zimbabwe), Southwest Africa (Nam-

ibia) and South Africa, their chosen method again being guerrilla warfare. Indeed, wherever the colonialists and/or the colonists (the settlers) resisted African nationalist demands, the nationalists adopted guerrilla warfare as a standard technique in their struggle for African liberation.

The first major guerrilla conflict in postwar Africa was the Mau Mau revolt in Kenya (1952-1960), though this was

arguably more a tribal insurrection than a genuinely nationalist campaign. Support for the Mau Mau was limited almost exclusively to the Kikuyu, plus the associated tribes of the Embu and Meru. True, the Kikuyu was Kenya's biggest tribe, numbering over 1,500,000 people by 1950, but it constituted a minority of the African population. Moreover, the revolt was limited to a fraction – only one-sixteenth – of Kenya's land area, being confined to the Kikuyu Reserve and adjoining areas, that is Central Province and the eastern parts of Rift Valley Province.

The origins of the revolt lay in the development of militant anti-colonial sentiments within the Kikuyu tribe. Kenya in 1952 was a British colony inhabited by 6,000,000 people: 5,500,000 Africans, 165,000 Asians and 55,000 Europeans. Political power lay with the imperial authorities, the British, while economically the territory was dominated by the white settlers and to a degree by the Asians. Opposition to this regime had arisen from African leaders. They complained of the influx of white settlers after World War II, of the growing economic disparities between whites and Africans and of the second- or even third-class status accorded to the Africans. The Kikuyu had the most developed sense of grievance. Their Reserve bordered on the capital, Nairobi, whence many Kikuyu had migrated and seen white wealth and prosperity. Their Reserve also bordered on the White Highlands, where settlers had developed thriving farms on land that the Kikuyu believed should by rights belong to them. This grievance was given greater impetus by worsening conditions in the Reserve, where overused land could no longer sustain a rapidly expanding population. Such factors led to growing disaffection among the Kikuyu, reflected in

**Top far left: A Kikuyu witch doctor.
Far left: Europeans demonstrate in Nairobi, January 1953, for a firmer stand against the Mau Mau.
Top: Erskine (center) observing operations against the Mau Mau.
Left: Jomo Kenyatta, founder of the KAU. Suspected by the British of instigating the Mau Mau revolt, he was detained.**

69

the rise of the Kenya African Union (KAU), a political party founded in 1946 by Kamau wa Ngengi (Jomo Kenyatta). It was also reflected in the emergence of the Mau Mau, a secret movement that sheltered behind the (legal) KAU. The Mau Mau aimed to eject the settlers, proselytize the entire Kikuyu tribe and set up an independent Kikuyu-dominated Kenya by violent means.

In October 1952, after a period of Mau Mau-inspired disturbances, the Governor of Kenya declared a State of Emergency and authorized certain emergency measures. By that time the Mau Mau threat was real enough. The movement's 'active wing,' which called itself the Land Freedom Army, had an estimated 12,500 guerrillas, based mainly in the forested areas of the Aberdare Mountains and Mount Kenya. The 'active wing' was supported by a 'passive wing,' based in the Reserve and Nairobi and estimated to be 30,000 strong; its role was to supply food, funds, Intelligence, recruits and weapons to the guerrillas. The insurgency was directed, in theory at least, by the Central Committee in Nairobi and through district committees in the Reserve and forested areas. Only a small proportion of the guerrillas – perhaps no more than 12 percent at that time – possessed firearms; the insurgents used clubs, knives, pangas or axes. They also used 'oathing' as a weapon. At the time the Kikuyu had a belief in the efficacy of magic, and in the killing power of oaths, and the Mau Mau exploited these beliefs for their own ends. Most of the Kikuyu were persuaded or coerced into taking some kind of oath. By this means the Mau Mau hoped to control their adherents and to intimidate those who were reluctant to co-operate.

Initially the Mau Mau met with some success. At the start of the Emergency the British had few troops in Kenya and little information about the movement's organization or strength. Consequently the guerrillas were able to impose a reign of terror. Between the start of the Emergency and mid-February 1953 they killed nine Europeans, three Asians and 177 Africans, with relative impunity. On 20 March 1953 they scored further successes. One Mau Mau gang raided Naivasha police station, killing two

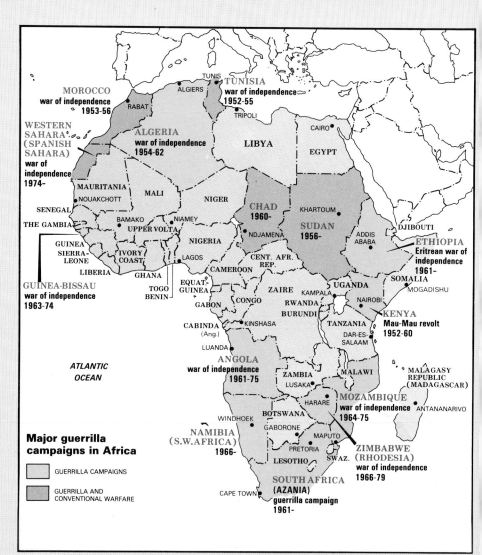

Major guerrilla campaigns in Africa

GUERRILLA CAMPAIGNS

GUERRILLA AND CONVENTIONAL WARFARE

MOROCCO war of independence 1953-56

TUNISIA war of independence 1952-55

WESTERN SAHARA (SPANISH SAHARA) war of independence 1974-

ALGERIA war of independence 1954-62

CHAD 1960-

SUDAN 1956-

ETHIOPIA Eritrean war of independence 1961-

GUINEA-BISSAU war of independence 1963-74

KENYA Mau-Mau revolt 1952-60

ANGOLA war of independence 1961-75

MOZAMBIQUE war of independence 1964-75

NAMIBIA (S.W.AFRICA) 1966-

ZIMBABWE (RHODESIA) war of independence 1966-79

SOUTH AFRICA (AZANIA) guerrilla campaign 1961-

Far left: An assortment of homemade firearms used by the Mau Mau.
Above: A Mau Mau camp in Meruland.
Left: A Mau Mau guerrilla surrenders.
Map: Guerrilla campaigns in Africa.

policemen, stealing 47 weapons and freeing 173 prisoners, while another gang – over 1000 strong – attacked the Kikuyu village of Lari, just north of Nairobi, hacking to death over 80 people (most of whom were women and children), mutilating 31 others, burning 200 huts and maiming 1000 cattle. The latter attack set the pattern for the Mau Mau campaign both in terms of the techniques used and the victims chosen. Gruesome attacks on animals as well as humans became commonplace and ghastly mutilations became a trademark of the Mau Mau insurgents. That the victims of the Lari massacre were Kikuyu was also typical, in that the vast majority of guerrilla attacks were

directed against fellow Kikuyu. Indeed, what was supposedly a campaign against the colonial authorities and white settlers quickly degenerated into a Kikuyu civil war.

The reason for this was that the Mau Mau lacked genuine popular support. The guerrilla campaign attracted virtually no support outside the Kikuyu tribal grouping and even within the tribe there was substantial opposition to the methods and even the objectives of the guerrillas, especially from tribal elders and Christians. Nearly all the Mau Mau were Kikuyu, but by no means all the Kikuyu were Mau Mau – while the guerrillas were eventually to attract 15,000 recruits, the Kikuyu Home Guard, set up by the British early in 1953, soon gained 20,000 volunteers. Nor did the Mau Mau gain much international support. This isolation meant, among other things, that arms could not be brought in from abroad, a major drawback considering that the guerrillas were rarely

able to capture weapons from the Security Forces after the Naivasha raid. Moreover, the Mau Mau campaign was soon threatened by British counter-measures. Within a year of the start of the troubles, the British had deployed five British and six King's African Rifles battalions. These forces, together with the Kenya Regiment, auxiliary forces and units of the Royal Air Force totalled about 10,000 men, while the police forces totalled about 20,000 and the Home Guard a similar number. The British proceeded to mount an effective counterinsurgency (COIN) campaign, establishing a trinity system of command (with a view to co-ordinating the activities of the army, police and civil administration) and isolating the Mau Mau by a program of political and economic reforms combined with military offensives.

By mid-1954 the Mau Mau were losing the initiative. In April of that year the Security Forces launched Operation

Anvil, a month-long cordon-and-search operation aimed at clearing the Mau Mau's underground organization from Nairobi. Over 16,500 suspects were detained, with hooded informers being used to identify Mau Mau members. Anvil proved to be a decisive blow. It destroyed the Mau Mau's influence within the capital, cut off the insurgents in the forests from their high command and source of supply in Nairobi, and produced much-needed Intelligence for the Security Forces.

The British followed up Anvil by clearing the Reserve of Mau Mau adherents, notably by resettling 'loyal' Kikuyu so as to deny food, shelter and Intelligence to the guerrillas. Finally the Security Forces switched their attention to the forests, the Prohibited Areas where there was no requirement to observe the common law. By use of aerial bombing, massive cordon-and-search operations, patrols and ambushes, together with pseudo- or counter-gangs

Above: French soldiers in the Aurès, Algeria, 1954.
Far left: Africans rounded-up by the police await 'screening,' Nairobi, 1953.

(consisting of loyal Africans and 'turned' guerrillas, posing as Mau Mau members), the British reduced the insurgents to small, disjointed and disorganized groups totalling no more than 2000 fighters by late 1955. A year later the insurgents had ceased to be a serious threat. The Emergency lasted officially until January 1960, though this was more to legitimize the continued detention of suspects than for operational purposes.

The Mau Mau campaign had failed. The guerrillas had killed nearly 2000 civilians and 600 members of the Security Forces, the vast majority in both cases being fellow Kikuyu. However, the guerrillas themselves had lost 11,500 killed and had failed either to drive out the white settlers or to convert the Kikuyu tribe and take over Kenya. All the same, the Mau Mau could claim to have accelerated Kenya's progress toward African self-government. In order to counter the guerrillas, Britain

had pushed through a series of political reforms which the white settlers might otherwise have been unwilling to accept. Africans were given greater political power and eventually, in December 1963, political control over an independent state of Kenya. That state, ironically, was led by none other than Jomo Kenyatta, who had been imprisoned during the Emergency as a suspected instigator of the Mau Mau campaign.

By the time the Mau Mau revolt had been suppressed, a large-scale insurgency was under way in another African country: the vast North African territory of Algeria. Algeria was then a French colony administered as an integral part of the French state. Unlike most of France's imperial possessions, it had become a colony in the true sense of the word, in that the population of 9,000,000, though overwhelmingly Moslem (Arab and Berber), included nearly 1,000,000 European settlers.

Known as *colons* or *pieds noirs* these settlers wielded political power in the territory and were determined to keep it French. So too were many people in metropolitan France, a sentiment epitomized in the slogan *Algérie Française*.

Some Moslems also endorsed *Algérie Française*, but others did not. During the late 1940s and early 1950s increasing opposition to French colonialism had developed. Three broad strands of Algerian nationalism had emerged: the Islamic fundamentalist Association des Ulemas, the liberal Union Démocratique pour le Manifeste Algérien (UDMA) led by Ferhat Abbas, and the more radical Mouvement pour la Triomphe des Libertés Démocratiques (MTLD) led by Messali Hadj. The most militant party, however, was the

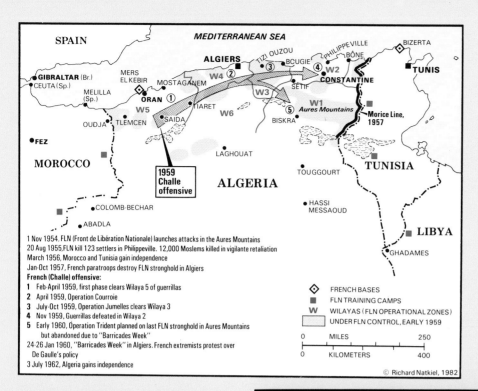

1 Nov 1954, FLN (Front de Libération Nationale) launches attacks in the Aures Mountains
20 Aug 1955, FLN kill 123 settlers in Philippeville. 12,000 Moslems killed in vigilante retaliation
March 1956, Morocco and Tunisia gain independence
Jan-Oct 1957, French paratroops destroy FLN stronghold in Algiers
French (Challe) offensive:
1 Feb-April 1959, first phase clears Wilaya 5 of guerrillas
2 April 1959, Operation Courroie
3 July-Oct 1959, Operation Jumelles clears Wilaya 3
4 Nov 1959, Guerrillas defeated in Wilaya 2
5 Early 1960, Operation Trident planned on last FLN stronghold in Aures Mountains
    but abandoned due to "Barricades Week"
24-26 Jan 1960, "Barricades Week" in Algiers. French extremists protest over
De Gaulle's policy
3 July 1962, Algeria gains independence

◇ FRENCH BASES
■ FLN TRAINING CAMPS
W WILAYAS (FLN OPERATIONAL ZONES)
☐ UNDER FLN CONTROL, EARLY 1959

0   MILES   250
0   KILOMETERS   400

© Richard Natkiel, 1982

Organisation Spéciale (OS), formed by hard-liners who had broken away from the MTLD in 1949. It was from the OS that Ahmed Ben Bella and other leaders emerged to create a revolutionary movement dedicated to organizing the 'liberation' of Algeria. By October 1954 the new movement had assumed the title Fronte de Libération Nationale (FLN).

From the outset the FLN's campaign was directed by a collective leadership comprising at first nine men; care was taken to give representation to both the Arab and Berber components of Algeria's Moslem community. The FLN's leaders also agreed at the outset to a second principle from which the FLN never wavered: that they must fight on relentlessly until independence was achieved. To this end, they divided Algeria into six autonomous zones or *Wilayas*. *Wilaya* 1 was the Aurès; *Wilaya* 2 the area around Philippeville and Constantine; *Wilaya* 3 the Kabylia; *Wilaya* 4 the area around Algiers (the Algérois); *Wilaya* 5 the area around Oran (the Oranie); and *Wilaya* 6 the hinterland behind the Algérois. The date for a general uprising was set for 1 November 1954, when several hundred FLN guerrillas, armed mostly with weapons abandoned in North Africa during World War II, were to launch selected attacks against French targets in each *Wilaya*. Some FLN leaders, like

Belkacem Krim, were to lead the revolt, while others, like Ben Bella, were to seek support from potentially sympathetic governments, particularly in the Arab world.

The FLN's campaign got off to a bad start. Many of the attacks were bungled and the French, despite the fact that they had few regular troops in Algeria, managed to kill or arrest many nationalist leaders. By February 1955 the FLN was in some difficulty. One of its leaders – Mourad Didouche – was dead, two others – Mostafa Ben Boulaid and Rabah Bitat – had fallen into French hands, and the movement was down to less than 350 active guerrillas. Nevertheless, the FLN survived and as fresh recruits came forward the guerrilla networks were gradually rebuilt. Moreover the FLN succeeded in negating French reforms aimed at undercutting support for the insurgents. On 20 August 1955 guerrillas attacked villages in the Philippeville (now called Skikda) area, butchering *pied noir* men, women and children in the most horrific manner. The *pieds noirs*, on their part, retaliated by murdering thousands of Moslems. This massacre of Moslems played into the hands of the FLN, since it not only shocked international and French public opinion but in Algeria itself drove a wedge between European and Moslem which was never really removed.

During the following year or so the FLN's position improved markedly, despite a rapid build-up of French forces. In March 1956 the French granted independence to their troubled protectorates of Morocco and Tunisia. This enabled the French government to concentrate its resources in Algeria, but it also helped the FLN, since the independence of Algeria's western and eastern neighbors opened up the possibility of acquiring safe base areas for the guerrillas. Indeed, by the end of the year both Morocco and particularly Tunisia were being used as sanctuaries and conduits for supplies and arms. The FLN also made advances within Algeria itself. The movement's political platform – fervently nationalistic and broadly Islamic and socialist – had strong appeal, and the message reached a wider audience after the establishment in 1956 of an FLN newspaper and radio station.

Far left, top: Key features of the FLN war in Algeria.
Left: Ahmed Ben Bella of the FLN after his arrest. The civilian aircraft in which Ben Bella was travelling from Rabat to Tunis was intercepted by the **French and forced to land in Algiers, October 1956.**
Top left: French troops occupy a makeshift observation post, Algiers, 1958.
Above: General Massu's paras carrying out a routine search in the Casbah, Algiers, January 1957.

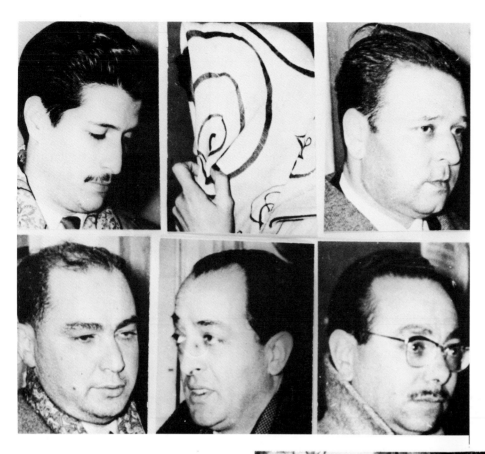

The movement attracted new recruits from uncommitted Moslems and from rival parties like the UDMA and the Mouvement Nationaliste Algérienne (MNA), the successor to the MTLD. Indeed, by mid-1956 the FLN had either absorbed or eliminated its chief rivals, including the UDMA, MNA and the Parti Communiste Algérien (PCA), and had transformed itself into a mass movement. The FLN also benefitted from being completely reorganized. In particular the military command structure was overhauled. The movement's rather disparate guerrilla groups were brought under central control and formed into the Armée de Libération Nationale (ALN), which like the FLN had both an internal and an external wing; the latter was based in Tunisia and was given the task of supporting the guerrilla teams operating inside Algeria. The whole politico-military effort was given central direction by the creation of a new supreme body called the Comité de Coordination et d'Execution (CCE). This body included the only two leaders of the original nine still at large – Krim and Larbi Ben M'hidi – and one of the new, somewhat more militant leaders, Ramdane Abane.

Top: FLN leaders arrested in metropolitan France. France's large community of Algerian immigrants was regarded by the FLN as a source of funds and support.
Top right: French soldiers taken prisoner by the nationalists.

Above: FLN officers plan an ambush on a French patrol.
Right: An FLN ambush team, photographed by a journalist allowed to wander freely in an FLN camp.

Advances notwithstanding, the FLN was to suffer a series of devastating military setbacks after 1956, for the French, determined to avoid any more defeats like those in 1940 (against the Germans) and 1954 (against the Viet Minh) had poured in 500,000 troops and were pursuing a comprehensive COIN strategy under the doctrine of *guerre révolutionnaire*. The first major blow came within the city of Algiers, where the FLN had built up a powerful urban terrorist network. In September 1956 the FLN ordered its political leaders in Algiers, Ben M'hidi and his lieutenant Saadi Yacef, to initiate a systematic terror campaign there. Yacef's 1400 or so activists, operating from the safety of the Casbah (a Moslem area of the city) soon set about their task. By the end of the year bombings and assassinations were an everyday occurrence. However, in January 1957, as FLN terrorism and *pied noir* counterterrorism threatened to plunge Algiers into anarchy, the local

authorities handed over complete authority to the Army, in the shape of General Jacques Massu's 10th Colonial Parachute Division. *Les paras* proceeded to smash the FLN's network. Patrols, checkpoints and house-to-house searches were instigated, 'loyal' Moslems were detailed to report on suspicious activities and infiltrate FLN areas, and suspected FLN members were rounded up and subjected to 'deep interrogation' – they were tortured into revealing information about the FLN network in the city. These methods produced the intended results. Both Ben M'hidi and Yacef were captured and by October 1957 the FLN's network was destroyed. As the bombings stopped and the CCE's four surviving members fled to Tunis, internal dissension within the nationalist camp resurfaced and Moslem support for the FLN began to wane.

The FLN then suffered another major setback. Faced with guerrilla infiltration from Tunisia (the FLN's preferred ex-

ternal base) and to a lesser extent from Morocco, the French took measures to seal off both borders by creating impassable barriers stretching all the way from the Mediterranean Sea to the wastes of the Sahara Desert. On the border with Tunisia the French built an elaborate barrier called the Morice Line. This 320km (200-mile) line consisted of an electrified fence, barbed wire and minefields and was backed up by artillery, armor, aircraft and 80,000 troops. Completed in September 1957, the Morice Line and its equivalent on the Moroccan border cut off the internal FLN from its external wing and from its main source of weapons and supplies.

Worse still, from the FLN's point of view, was that the guerrilla campaign inside Algeria was faltering in the face of a highly effective French COIN campaign. The French had deployed 300,000 troops across the countryside in a *quadrillage* so as to protect the population. They had begun to resettle Moslems in 'safe areas.' They had improved social services and introduced a counter-propaganda campaign. They had infiltrated the ALN and exploited the numerous feuds that bedevilled the FLN – between the Arabs and Berbers and the internal and external wings, for example – and they had greatly enhanced their mobility by using helicopters on a large scale. These tactics bore fruit. During 1958 the ALN suffered heavy casualties and its active strength inside Algeria was reduced to perhaps 15,000 backed up by 30,000 irregulars. This strength was concen-

Above: A riot in Algiers, 1960.
Below right: Ahmed Ben Bella, independent Algeria's first president, visiting Cuba, 1962.
Top right: The GPRA executive at Rabat in March 1962.

trated in a few remaining strongholds, but in 1959 even these areas came under threat as the new French Commander-in-Chief, General Maurice Challe, launched a fresh offensive. Using pro-French Moslems (*harkis*) to locate the guerrillas, fast pursuit groups (Commandos de Chasse) to pin them down, and crack units of the Réserve Générale to eliminate them, Challe's forces combed one ALN stronghold after another with overwhelming force. By the end of 1959 the ALN had been reduced to scattered and demoralized groups totalling only 8000 men. Guerrilla activity was effectively limited to the Aurès, an area Challe planned to clear in early 1960.

But if the FLN was losing militarily, it was winning politically and diplomatically. The nationalists received moral support from the non-aligned states, got hearings at the United Nations (UN), and the FLN's provisional government, the Gouvernement Provisoire de la République Algérienne (GPRA), founded in September 1958, was recognized by the USSR, the Chinese People's Republic and states. In addition, the FLN was winning the political 'war' within France itself. Guerrilla atrocities may have been unspeakable, but by provoking *les colons* into appalling

78

retaliations and by forcing *les paras* to resort to the torture of detainees, the nationalists drove a wedge between Moslems and Europeans in Algeria, put France in the international dock and alienated French public opinion. Indeed, while many Frenchmen supported the stance of *Algérie Française*, others – a growing majority – became disenchanted, feeling that the war had become too costly in moral, political, economic and military terms. The unstable coalition governments of the Fourth Republic (1946-1958) failed either to take decisive steps toward victory or disengagement. Under the Fifth Republic (formed in 1958), however, France had a more stable regime and a leader, Charles de Gaulle, in a better position to choose.

De Gaulle chose to disengage, despite the fact that the proponents of *Algérie Française* had been instrumental in bringing him to power in June 1958. Indeed it gradually became evident that far from being a devotee of *Algérie Française*, de Gaulle saw the war as an obstacle to his plans to revive French economic and political power. On 16 September 1959 de Gaulle spoke of the need for Algerian self-determination. He subsequently called off the Challe offensive, ordered a unilateral ceasefire and opened up negotiations with the GPRA. These actions did not endear the new leader to supporters of *Algérie Française*, as *pied noir* disturbances in January 1960, an attempted *putsch* by army officers in April 1961 and various assassination attempts by the Organisation Armée Secrète (OAS) illustrated. However, de Gaulle persisted and, with a majority of Frenchmen behind him, negotiated a peace settlement with the FLN. The final agreement was signed at Evian in March 1962 and represented a total victory for the nationalists. De Gaulle abandoned claims to the oil and gas fields in the Sahara and demands that the *pieds noirs* be granted dual citizenship, and instead agreed to grant independence to Algeria, in July 1962, upon the FLN's terms. Thus the French, after eight years of war and the loss of 17,456 troops, withdrew from Algeria. So too did the *pieds noirs*. They left in droves, though the *harkis* were not so fortunate – many of them were to meet an atrocious fate at the hands of the FLN. As for the FLN, it had won a total political victory, despite continuous feuds and personal rivalries, and despite a series of military debacles. The cost, however, had been immense: according to the nationalists themselves, the Moslem population of Algeria had been reduced by over 1,000,000 during the course of the war.

The FLN's triumph in Algeria was subsequently paralleled by the success of African nationalists in Portuguese Africa. In all three of Portugal's mainland African territories – Angola, Mozambique and Guinea-Bissau – nationalist movements initiated guerrilla campaigns against the Portuguese in the early 1960s. The outcome of these wars was to be similar to that in Algeria. The nationalists did not defeat the imperial power militarily, but they succeeded in wearing down their adversary's resolve to continue the war. While the FLN's campaign brought about the collapse of the French Fourth Republic, the nationalist campaigns in Lusophone Africa precipitated the overthrow of the Salazar-Caetano regime and expedited the collapse of the Portuguese empire.

Portugal, the first of the European powers to establish itself in Africa, was the last to decide upon withdrawal. This reluctance to abandon its empire was based in part upon economic grounds, in that Portugal, as one of the poorest states in Western Europe, felt it could not afford to lose a potentially wealthy country like Angola. Equally, if not more important, were political considerations. The retention of vast overseas holdings conferred on Portugal an international status which a small and poor country could not otherwise have attained. The Portuguese did not see themselves as imperialists. They claimed that their overseas possessions formed an integral part of the Portuguese state, a claim given formal status in 1951 when these territories were declared 'overseas provinces' of Portugal. Moreover the Portuguese claimed to be fulfilling a unique 'civilizing' mission in Africa. True, the constitution of 1933 had divided the population of the African territories into two distinct categories, namely the *indigenas* (natives) and the *não-indigenas* (non-

natives), but the latter category included *mestiços* (half-castes) and *assimilados* (assimilated or 'civilized' Africans) as well as whites. In theory there was nothing to prevent a native from achieving the status of *assimilado* and thereby assuming the privileges and responsibilities of full Portuguese citizenship.

Nevertheless, Portuguese policies produced rising disaffection. Africans resented the contract labor system which forced them to produce cash crops and undermined subsistence farming. Wages were low and 'poor white' immigrants from Portugal were displacing natives from even menial jobs in Angola and Mozambique. Moreover, Africans complained of the lack of social services and educational facilities. The lack of schools was especially galling, since educational qualifications were needed in order to attain the status of *assimilado* – by 1961, in fact, barely one percent of Africans had reached this status. Above all else, perhaps, the Africans felt that the Portuguese were imposing an alien culture upon them.

During the late 1950s and early 1960s nationalist movements sprang up in each of Portugal's African territories, movements led, ironically, by *mestiços* and *assimilados*. In Guinea, a small, water-

logged and largely unpopulated West African country, the main party was the leftist Partido Africano da Independência da Guiné e Cabo Verde (PAIGC). Founded in 1956, the PAIGC was dominated by Cape Verdian *mestiços* such as Amilcar Cabral and drew most of its rank-and-file support from the Balante tribe, which comprised some 30 percent of the population of 800,000. In Mozambique, a much larger country with a sizeable settler population, the main party was the Frente de Libertação de Moçambique (FRELIMO), a coalition of several groups that united in 1962 under the leadership of Eduardo Mondlane. FRELIMO was based upon the Makonde tribe of northern Mozambique, though many of its leaders were from other parts of the country. In Angola, a large, mineral-rich territory with several hundred thousand settlers, the political situation was more complicated. Three nationalist movements had emerged. One was the Movimento Popular de Libertação de Angola (MPLA), a Marxist party founded in 1956. The MPLA tried to attract support from all tribes and races, although in practice its rank-and-file was drawn mainly from the Mbundu tribe that lived in and around Luanda, while its leader-

ship was dominated by *mestiços* like Viriato da Cruz and *assimilados* like Agostinho Neto. By contrast the rival União das Populacoes de Angola (UPA), founded in 1954 and led by Holden Roberto, drew its support almost exclusively from the Bakongo tribe of northwestern Angola; later, in 1962, the UPA renamed itself the Frente de Libertação de Angola (FNLA). Roberto's lieutenant Jonas Savimbi broke away to form a third party, the União Nacional para a Independência Total de Angola (UNITA) in 1966, a movement that relied mainly on the Ovimbundu and Chokwe tribes of southern and eastern Angola. All three Angolan movements,

Far left: Luiz Cabral (right), leader of the PAIGC.
Left: Agostinho Neto (left) of the MPLA, who became president of the Angolan People's Republic in 1975.
Below: An FNLA camp in Zaire, occupied by guerrillas and refugees.

like their counterparts in Mozambique
and Guinea, decided to wage guerrilla
wars against the Portuguese.

The first of the three territories to
experience such warfare was Angola. In
March 1961 UPA guerrillas, armed with
machetes and other weapons, massacred
and mutilated several hundred white
settlers and several thousand blacks,
mestiços and *assimilados* in northwestern
Angola. The whole region, dominated
by the Bakongo tribe, was soon in the

throes of a bloody and widespread rebellion. The rival MPLA began its
campaign during 1963-64 and UNITA
followed suit in 1966. By that time
guerrilla offensives had already started
in both Guinea and Mozambique, with
the PAIGC opening its campaign in
January 1963 and FRELIMO launching
its first attacks in September 1964.

These guerrilla groups held a number
of advantages over the Portuguese.
When the revolts began, Portugal had

few troops in Africa – only 1000 in
Guinea and 3000 in Angola in 1961,
though in the case of Mozambique they
were better prepared, with 16,000 there
by 1964. Moreover the Portuguese had
had little recent experience of COIN, or
for that matter conventional warfare.
Another advantage accruing to the guerrillas was that the international climate
was strongly anticolonial. The UN
General Assembly gave moral support to
the nationalists, while the Organization

Left: An MPLA training camp in Angola, 1974. Political theory is taught alongside military instruction.

Below: Guerrillas of the FNLA undergoing weapons training at a camp in Zaire.

of African Unity (OAU) granted political recognition to the PAIGC, FRELIMO and, in Angola, the FNLA until 1968 and thereafter the MPLA. Furthermore, the guerrillas were able to use sanctuaries in adjacent states and attracted the material support of powerful governments. The PAIGC gained Soviet-bloc support and operated from bases in the neighboring countries of Guinea-Conakry and Senegal. FRELIMO was given help by both the USSR and the Chinese People's Republic and secured bases in Zambia and Tanzania. The FNLA found the ex-Belgian Congo (Zaire) a natural refuge, especially after Roberto's brother-in-law Joseph Mobutu became president. The FNLA received assistance from the Chinese and later tacit support from the Americans, who were hedging their bets against a Portuguese defeat. The Marxist MPLA was backed by the Soviet bloc and found sanctuary in the ex-French Congo (Congo-Brazzaville) and Zambia. UNITA was backed by China, though it had no external bases after being ejected from Zambia following attacks on the Benguela railroad, which was vital to Zambia's economy.

All the same, the Portuguese were not easily discouraged. They responded defiantly, pouring in troops and mounting a full-scale COIN campaign. Troop levels were raised from a few thousand in 1961 to 130,000 by 1964 and 150,000 by the early 1970s; these levels were reached by sending the bulk of the Portuguese Army to Africa and by recruiting more and more Africans in each of the three territories. Airplanes and helicopters were also dispatched, albeit on a limited scale, and these were used for, among other things, the interdiction of guerrilla supply routes. Hundreds of thousands of villagers were resettled in protected villages or *aldeamentos* so as to isolate the guerrillas from the people. Social services were expanded and the army used to build schools and clinics. Attempts were also made to undermine the nationalists' political appeal by treating all Africans as fully fledged Portuguese citizens – in 1961, after the outbreak of disturbances in Angola, the Portuguese abolished the distinction between *indigenas* and *não-indigenas* and introduced labor reforms.

These COIN policies, though in some respects unsuccessful, went a long way toward negating the efforts of the nationalists. None of the guerrilla groups found the going easy. In Angola the UPA/FNLA ran into difficulties at an early stage. The Portuguese, responding to the initial revolt with fire and sword, killed or drove over the Zairean border dozens of guerrillas and

Above: Samora Machel (right).
Right: Angolan children on the statue of Norton de matos, the Portuguese founder of Nova Lisboa (Huambo).

thousands of Bakongo tribesmen, re-establishing control over most of north-western Angola by October 1961. The FNLA survived, but in reality its fighting strength was perhaps only 6000 and its campaign rather desultory, being limited to forays from Zaire and from the Dembos Mountains within Angola. Indeed, in 1968 the OAU withdrew recognition from the FNLA and threw its support behind the rival MPLA. The MPLA was certainly more active militarily but it fared little better. The MPLA's initial strategy, that of infiltrating from Congo-Brazzaville into the Cabinda enclave, had to be abandoned because local support was lacking. Switching to Zambian bases, the MPLA opened up new fronts in 1967-68 by infiltrating the eastern and central districts of Moxico and Bié. This proved more successful, but the guerrillas were rarely able to reach the Mbundu heartland around Luanda and only a minority of the MPLA's 5000-7000 guerrillas were able to operate permanently inside Angola. UNITA, not having an external base, did operate inside Angola, but its

Left: By independence a war of succession had broken out between MPLA and the combined forces of UNITA and the FNLA in Angola. Above: UNITA leader, Jonas Savimbi.

strength was limited to a few hundred and it was concerned more with political than military action.

FRELIMO too faced serious problems. The guerrillas found it difficult to extend their operations beyond the Makonde-dominated Mueda plateau in the northeastern province of Cabo Delgado, because the area to the south was inhabited by the Macua tribe (40 percent of the entire population of Mozambique), who were hostile to the Makonde and remained pro-Portuguese. The guerrillas managed to penetrate Niassa province in 1967, where the Nyaja tribe proved co-operative, but this was offset by the willingness of the local Yao tribe to back the Portuguese. Consequently, guerrilla activities were confined mostly to the north of the country, and, as in Angola, consisted mainly of hit-and-run attacks and minelaying. There were further setbacks in 1968 when FRELIMO guerrillas failed to interrupt seriously the work on the vital Cabora Bassa Dam project in Tete province, and in 1969 when internal feuding within the movement climaxed in the assassination of Mondlane and his replacement by the pro-Soviet Marxist Samora Machel. FRELIMO did make

advances during the early 1970s, establishing itself in Tete province and penetrating to the south and east in late 1973, but the Portuguese were far from beaten. Even in Guinea, where the guerrillas were relatively successful, the Portuguese managed to force a military stalemate. The PAIGC had secured control of over 60 percent of the country by the late 1960s and established 'liberated zones.' Even so, tribes such as the Fula and Mandinka (which together made up nearly a quarter of the population) remained pro-Portuguese and the socio-economic reforms pursued by General Antonio de Spinóla undercut nationalist support.

In all three territories, however, the nationalists were ultimately to triumph. Military successes notwithstanding, the Portuguese gradually became more and more disenchanted with the African wars since these were costly in terms of both blood and treasure. Guerrilla losses were heavy, but the Portuguese suffered too, losing perhaps 11,000 dead and 30,000 wounded by 1974. Many of the casualties were young conscripts – in the late 1960s, despite the progressive 'Africanization' of the wars, the Portuguese had been compelled to lower the age of conscription and extend the period of national service in order to prosecute the wars. The economic costs were also high. The proportion of the national budget devoted to defense rose from 25 percent in 1960 to over 40 percent in 1968, a heavy burden for one of the West's most impoverished countries. Considerations such as these eventually led to a reappraisal of Portuguese policy. On 25 April 1974 the radical Movimento das Forças Armadas (MFA or Armed Forces Movement) launched a *coup d'état* in Lisbon, toppling the regime of Marcello Caetano. Among the MFA's prime objectives was that of finding a political solution to the African wars. The new head of government, General Spinóla, talked in terms of granting greater autonomy to the 'overseas provinces' within a federal structure. Within six months of the coup, however, Spinóla had been ousted by leaders with a more radical outlook who decided on a rapid and unconditional withdrawal from empire. Guinea was given independence in

Right: African women singing the praises of Jonas Savimbi at a UNITA camp in southeastern Angola, 1977.
Far right: A march-past by members of the MPLA government's Organization of National Defense, Angola.
Bottom right: UNITA guerrillas armed with Chinese weapons, Angola, 1977.
Below: By February 1976 the MPLA controlled most of Angola. UNITA refused to accept defeat and fought the MPLA and its Cuban backers. Here UNITA personnel attack in southern Angola, 1977.

September 1974, under the PAIGC. Mozambique followed in June 1975, under a FRELIMO government. Angola received independence in November 1975, though by that time the country was in the throes of a war of succession between the MPLA and FNLA/UNITA. The MPLA, backed by Soviet arms and Cuban ground forces, had by early 1976 defeated its enemies in a largely conventional war.

The accession to power of the MPLA in Angola and FRELIMO in Mozambique had a profound effect on the course of three other guerrilla campaigns that had already begun in the region: the struggles for black majority rule in the British colony of Rhodesia (later called Zimbabwe), the South African-administered territory of Southwest Africa (referred to by the nationalists as Namibia) and in the white-ruled independent state of South Africa (referred to by the nationalists as Azania). While the Portuguese remained in Angola and Mozambique, all three territories had been insulated, to a considerable degree, from guerrilla attack. However, the MPLA and FRELIMO victories tilted the scales against the white supremacists. These victories not only gave a tremendous psychological boost to the Zimbabwean, Namibian and Azanian nationalists but opened up new possibilities for the guerrillas, in that all three white-ruled territories were now dangerously exposed. The guerrillas were not slow to exploit the new openings; Rhodesia in particular soon felt the consequences.

African nationalist movements had begun to emerge in Rhodesia (known as Southern Rhodesia until Northern Rhodesia became independent as Zambia in 1964) in the late 1950s and early 1960s, when the territory formed part of the British-sponsored Central African Federation (CAF). The first major African nationalist party was the African National Congress (ANC), established in 1957 by Joshua Nkomo. Its successor, the National Democratic Party (NDP) was much more militant. Founded in January 1960 by Nkomo, Herbert Chitepo, the Reverend Ndabaningi Sithole and Robert Mugabe, it demanded independence under a one-man one-vote system of

Right: Zimbabwean nationalists stage a procession to celebrate the break-up of the Federation of Rhodesia and Nyasaland. The coffin contains a mock body of the Federation's former prime minister, Sir Roy Welensky.
Below: Southern Rhodesian policemen on a flag-showing march through the township of Harare, Salisbury, October 1962.

government. The NDP was to be disappointed, however, because in 1961 Britain decided to grant Southern Rhodesia a new constitution that provided not for immediate majority rule but for a very gradual movement in that direction. The British were not unsympathetic to nationalist demands, but their position was complicated by the fact that Southern Rhodesia, unlike its federation partners – Northern Rhodesia and Nyasaland – was dominated economically and politically by white settlers. The territory had been governed by white settlers since 1923 and the white community, which by the early 1960s numbered 220,000 out of a total population of 4,250,000, was determined to keep things that way. Indeed, as the African nationalists clamored for majority rule the whites, fearing for their privileges and their safety, voted into power the Rhodesian Front (RF), a new political party dedicated to keeping power in 'civilized' hands. The RF soon cracked down on the nationalists. The NDP had been succeeded by two parties, the Zimbabwe African People's Union (ZAPU), led by Nkomo, and the Zimbabwe African National Union (ZANU), led by Sithole – both were outlawed and their leaders detained in 1964. The RF also took on the British, who in 1964 had granted independence to both Northern Rhodesia (Zambia) and Nyasaland (Malawi) under majority rule systems. When the British insisted that as a precondition to independence Rhodesia would have to grant the Africans a greater say in government, the RF retaliated by seizing independence. This Unilateral Declaration of Independence (UDI) was announced by Rhodesian premier Ian Smith on 11 November 1965.

Britain attempted to reverse UDI by imposing diplomatic and economic sanctions against Rhodesia so as to make the RF negotiate an acceptable settlement. This policy continued for 14 years, but the African nationalists, on their part, preferred from the outset to use more forceful methods. Soon after UDI they began a guerrilla campaign. From their headquarters in Zambia both ZAPU and ZANU beamed radio broadcasts to Rhodesia, urging Africans to revolt. They then sent small groups of guerrillas, who

Above: Joshua Nkomo seen here under detention at Gonakudzingwa, February 1965.

Top right: Bishop Abel Muzorewa, Rhodesia's first black prime minister.
Top left: The Reverend Ndabaningi Sithole, founder of ZANU.

Top center: Robert Mugabe deposed Sithole as ZANU leader and gained an overwhelming victory in the 1980 election.

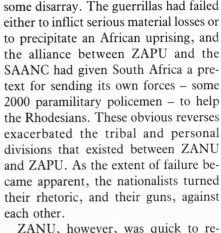

Above: British and Rhodesian premiers Harold Wilson (left) and Ian Smith (right) after talks on independence, London, October 1965. Below: Prime Minister Harold Wilson (second left) meets ZANU members, Salisbury, October 1965.

had been trained during the preceding years in various African and Eastern-bloc countries, across the border into Rhodesia. Facing them on the south side of the Zambezi River was a small Rhodesian army, with only 3400 regulars (1000 of whom were black), backed by a few dozen aircraft – Vampires, Hunters, Canberras and Alouette helicopters.

The first serious incursion occurred in April 1966, when a group of 14 ZANU insurgents went south with orders to sabotage power lines and attack white farms. The insurgents were none too successful. They managed to kill a white farmer and his wife, but all were subsequently killed or captured; the same fate befell other insurgents who infiltrated later that year. Larger groups which entered Rhodesia during 1967 and 1968 fared no better. In August 1967 a force of 90 guerrillas belonging to ZAPU and the South African African National Congress (SAANC) crossed the frontier near Victoria Falls. Its presence was reported by local tribesmen and most of the insurgents were eliminated. A second joint force was located and decimated in March-April 1968, as was a third that entered during July. By the end of 1968 more than 160 guerrillas had been killed for the loss of only 12 members of the Security Forces.

By that time the nationalists were in

some disarray. The guerrillas had failed either to inflict serious material losses or to precipitate an African uprising, and the alliance between ZAPU and the SAANC had given South Africa a pretext for sending its own forces – some 2000 paramilitary policemen – to help the Rhodesians. These obvious reverses exacerbated the tribal and personal divisions that existed between ZANU and ZAPU. As the extent of failure became apparent, the nationalists turned their rhetoric, and their guns, against each other.

ZANU, however, was quick to recover. Recognizing that the incursions of 1966-68 had been disastrous, it attempted to rectify its mistakes. In April 1969 ZANU's exiled leaders set up an eight-member war council called the *Dare re Chimurenga*, with a view to organizing a Maoist-style protracted war designed to wear down the Rhodesian government's human and economic resources. Chinese instructors were brought into the camps in Tanzania to train recruits to the Zimbabwe African National Liberation Army (ZANLA). ZANU also decided to establish new infiltration routes. Its target was to be northeastern Rhodesia, where the authorities were unpopular with the local Shona people. ZANU persuaded FRELIMO to allow ZANLA guerrillas to operate out of FRELIMO-dominated areas in Mozambique's Tete province – the area adjoining northeastern Rhodesia. It won over the local Africans, notably by enlisting the support of spirit mediums – who still hold great sway in the area – and established arms caches. Having thus prepared the ground, ZANU launched its new campaign in December 1972.

The Rhodesians, though initially taken by surprise, gradually implemented a series of countermeasures. The Security Forces swept guerrilla-affected areas, crossed the border into Mozambique (with Portugal's consent) and set up a border minefield or *cordon sanitaire* along parts of that border. They offered rewards to villagers for information about the guerrillas and imposed collective fines on villages suspected of helping the insurgents. They also began to move some villagers into protected villages (PVs) so as to isolate them from the guer-

rillas. Some of these COIN measures were counterproductive, but in the short-term at least they worked. The guerrillas were gradually eliminated, losing over 500 men during 1973 and 1974, compared with only 58 dead for the Security Forces. By the end of 1974 less than 100 hard-core guerrillas remained at large.

If the guerrillas were losing the 'shooting war,' there were compensations. In order to mount the COIN campaign in the northeast, the Rhodesians had had to extend the period of national service, call up Coloreds and Asians (who were previously exempt), activate a large number of white reservists and recruit Africans; their human resources were being stretched. Moreover the guerrillas were provided with a respite at this juncture by political developments. The South Africans, having given the RF government economic and military help during the first eight years of UDI, decided to disengage themselves. Mozambique was about to come under an African govern-

Above: A white Rhodesian woman being trained to use firearms.
Below: Rhodesian nationalist guerrillas.

Right: Muzorewa (left), Smith (second left), Chirau (second right) and Sithole sign a settlement allowing for black majority rule, March 1978.

ment, thus exposing Rhodesia's 1300km (800-mile) eastern border to guerrilla infiltration. Calculating that the RF regime had become militarily untenable without open-ended support, the South Africans decided that their interests would best be served by promoting a peaceful settlement. Zambia too was eager for peace, since her support for the Zimbabwean cause had cost her dearly. Consequently South Africa and Zambia worked in tandem, the former using its influence to make Smith release gaoled nationalists, the latter, plus Tanzania, pressing the nationalists to negotiate. A ceasefire was ordered in December 1974, South Africa pulled out its forces in August 1975 and negotiations began.

The talks were fruitless, much to the chagrin of the sponsors, and the nationalist movements reverted to armed struggle. At this stage, however, the nationalists were unable to prosecute a successful offensive. ZANU was divided by a leadership struggle between Sithole and Mugabe; in the bush ZANLA morale sagged and casualties rocketed. ZAPU, now the sole beneficiary of Zambian sanctuary (ZANU had been expelled) was making no effective military contribution. Its military wing, the Zimbabwe People's Revolutionary Army (ZIPRA), was still in embryonic state and its leader, Nkomo, entered into bilateral talks with Smith in December 1975.

Over the following three years, however, the nationalists made great advances. ZAPU, and to a lesser extent ZANU, participated from time to time in settlement talks, but both intensified their guerrilla campaigns; clashes between the two were reduced when Nkomo and Mugabe, now the undisputed leader of ZANU, came together in late 1976 to form a loose alliance called the Patriotic Front (PF). ZANLA was strengthened by thousands of new recruits from the Shona tribes who were trained mainly in Tanzania and Mozambique, equipped with Soviet and Chinese weapons and based in Mozambique. ZANLA extended its operations throughout eastern Rhodesia (Mashonaland). ZIPRA, strengthened by an influx of Ndebele recruits, trained mainly in Angola and Zambia, lavishly equipped by the Soviet bloc and based in Zambia and Botswana, stepped up its activities in western Rhodesia (Matabeleland). The Rhodesian government, faced with this surge of guerrilla activi-

ties across the entire country, was compelled to place the country on a war footing. It extended national service, called up older white reservists and recruited more and more Africans and foreigners. It also stepped up the COIN campaign: imposing dusk-to-dawn curfews in many of the African Tribal Trust Lands (TTLs); extending the protected villages *cordon sanitaire* programs; and ordering cross-border raids on guerrilla camps in Mozambique, Zambia, Botswana and even Angola. Guerrilla casualties were massive, but the nationalists made good their losses and kept on fighting. They attacked farms, PVs, communications, mission stations and government installations and managed either by persuasion or sheer terror to establish control over many African areas. As local administration broke down, the economy faltered and white emigration increased and the RF government became increasingly desperate. Eventually it decided to take a political initiative. In an attempt to undermine the PF's political appeal and assuage international opinion, the Smith government negotiated a settlement with African leaders who shared its distaste for the PF – Sithole, Senator

93

Chief Jeremiah Chirau and Bishop Abel Muzorewa. One-man one-vote elections were held and the victor, Muzorewa, was sworn in as Rhodesia's first black prime minister in June 1979.

This 'internal settlement' did not end the war. The PF denounced the new premier as an RF puppet and intensified its insurgency campaign. The new government, on its part, intensified the COIN campaign it had inherited from the RF regime. Both sides were soon to reconsider their positions, however. The government's Security Forces, though inflicting huge losses on the guerrillas, were stretched to the limit. Their adversaries were over 10,000 strong and growing stronger every week; not even South African assistance, which had resumed by this time, could stem the tide. The PF also had problems. The so-called 'front-line' states, especially Zambia and Mozambique, were desperate for a peace settlement – their economies were in tatters as a result of Rhodesian cross-border raids. Consequently, when the British government made fresh settlement proposals, both sides responded positively. A ceasefire came into effect on 28 December 1979, a Commonwealth Monitoring Force flew in to supervise

Above: South African Alouette III helicopter in Namibia.
Below: Major General Acland (center), the commander of the Commonwealth Monitoring force.

Below: British troops in the Rhodesian bush. In accordance with the settlement terms agreed at Lancaster House a Commonwealth Monitoring Force supervised the ceasefire.

Left: South African troops inspect the bodies of dead guerrillas – 'floppies' – in Namibia.
Below: A SWAPO guerrilla taken prisoner in Namibia.

the ceasefire and fresh elections were held. The result, much to the consternation of Muzorewa and his white backers, was a clear victory for the PF: ZANU in Mashonaland and ZAPU in Matabeleland. The majority of seats went to ZANU and on 18 April 1980 Rhodesia became independent, as Zimbabwe, under a self-proclaimed Marxist, Robert Mugabe. The nationalists had been in many respects militarily incompetent, but they had excelled at political warfare. The result was reflected in a clear political victory at the ballot box.

If the year 1966 marked the beginning of systematic guerrilla operations in Rhodesia, it also saw the start of a guerrilla campaign in Southwest Africa, a vast, sparsely populated but mineral-rich country ruled by South Africa. This territory had first come under South African control during World War I, when South African units had seized the then-German colony of Süd West Afrika. After the war the territory was entrusted to South Africa under a 'C-class' League of Nations mandate, meaning that Pretoria could administer it as an integral part of South Africa.

Pretoria did so, and after the demise of the League in 1946 tightened its grip on the territory. The South Africans governed Southwest Africa under a modified form of their own *apartheid* (racial segregation) system, allowing the white community (14 percent of the population) to retain control over the southern two-thirds of the country and offering the ten non-white ethnic groups a form of self-government in separate 'homelands,' mainly in the north of the territory. By 1969 Southwest Africa was a *de facto* fifth province of South Africa.

South African policies were challenged, however, by the UN and by nationalists. Having succeeded the League of Nations, the UN passed numerous resolutions after 1946 urging Pretoria to place the territory under UN Trusteeship pending full independence. In the late 1960s the UN went further, revoking South Africa's mandate over the territory in October 1966 and renaming the territory Namibia in June 1968; three years later the International Court of Justice declared Pretoria's presence in Namibia to be illegal. In the meantime Namibia's African nationalists had decided to resort to guerrilla

warfare in order to oust the South Africans. The main nationalist movement was the South West Africa People's Organization (SWAPO), a party founded in April 1960 by Sam Nujoma and based on the populous Ovambo tribe, which by the mid-1960s numbered 270,000, roughly 46 percent of the entire population (SWAPO had begun life in 1957 as the Ovamboland People's Congress). During the early 1960s SWAPO had sent recruits off to various African and Eastern-bloc countries for guerrilla training. The first batch of trained guerrillas returned in late 1965 and established camps in the center-north of the territory – Ovamboland. Conflict began in August 1966, when units of the South African Police (SAP) attacked one of these camps.

During the next few years SWAPO made little headway. Few trained insurgents were available, SWAPO's strength being numbered in hundreds rather than thousands. Moreover, access to Namibia was a problem. From their bases in Zambia SWAPO guerrillas had to infiltrate either through southern Angola, which was under Portuguese control, or the Caprivi Strip, which was

Above: A park bench reserved for whites, Central Park, Johannesburg. Left: The bodies of black demonstrators killed at Sharpeville, South Africa, on 21 March 1960.

fortified and heavily patrolled by the SAP's paramilitary units. Up until 1974, indeed, SWAPO's military impact was negligible. Its military wing – the People's Liberation Army of Namibia (PLAN) – caused little damage and inflicted few casualties on the SAP or civilians. However, SWAPO's struggle was not altogether in vain. PLAN tied down several thousand South Africans, executed several spectacular attacks and caused real problems for the SAP by laying landmines in the Caprivi Strip after May 1971. Moreover SWAPO made progress on the political front. The SAP kept the nationalists off-balance by detaining some of their leaders (SWAPO was never banned outright in Namibia), but SWAPO's internal wing, by exploiting dissension caused by South African *apartheid* policies, built up a degree of popular support, especially in Ovamboland. Unrest in that area became so widespread that in February 1972 the

authorities were compelled to declare martial law. Pretoria also had to send in South African Defense Force (SADF) units, to relieve the overstretched SAP. By June 1974 the army had assumed official responsibility for all COIN operations along the border.

By that time things were beginning to go SWAPO's way. Portugal's withdrawal from Angola created new possibilities for PLAN, opening up a 1600km (1000-mile) long border to guerrilla infiltration. As the Portuguese pulled out of southern Angola, SWAPO set up bases there. Many of these bases were destroyed when the South Africans launched a brief intervention (August 1975-March 1976) in the Angolan civil war, but as the SADF withdrew from Angola, between January and March 1976, SWAPO soon re-established itself in the south of the country, with the blessing of the new MPLA regime. In the wake of the Angolan civil war, SWAPO's position improved markedly. Recruits flocked into the camps, pushing PLAN's strength up from 2000 in 1976 to 10,000 by 1978. These recruits were given better weapons, provided by the Soviet Union via Angola, and better

training, provided in Angola by Soviet, Cuban, East German and other Soviet-bloc personnel. In addition, SWAPO made advances on the international front. The UN General Assembly expressed moral support for SWAPO's armed struggle; by contrast, Pretoria was subjected to a UN-imposed arms embargo and continuous Western pressure to negotiate an internationally acceptable settlement. Thus strengthened, SWAPO intensified its campaign. Operations were extended to Ovamboland, Okavangoland and even to white farming areas to the south of the 'northern tier.' Targets included communications, power lines, government installations, pro-government blacks and the Security Forces.

The South Africans, however, proved to be stubborn and formidable foes. Pretoria, regarding Namibia as a vital buffer territory, was loath to let it fall under the sway of a Marxist-led nationalist group. Consequently the South Africans responded by devoting a substantial proportion of their military resources to Namibia. Troop levels were raised to 30,000 by deploying SADF regulars, conscripts, reservists and by recruiting local manpower, both white and black; these forces were backed by artillery, armor and aircraft, including helicopters. A full-scale COIN campaign was introduced and this had a socio-political as well as a military dimension – while some SADF units tracked down PLAN guerrillas, others implemented a civic action program, and the government itself instituted political reforms so as to undercut SWAPO's political appeal. Moreover the South Africans took the war to southern Angola, launching a series of devastating cross-border raids against SWAPO camps and weakening the MPLA regime by assisting UNITA – the latter had gone back to the bush and resumed hostilities against the MPLA after the civil war officially ended.

These policies tilted the military balance against SWAPO, frustrating successive attempts by PLAN to build up its forces for major offensives. They also made infiltration more difficult, because UNITA established control over most of southeastern Angola and the MPLA government, under intense

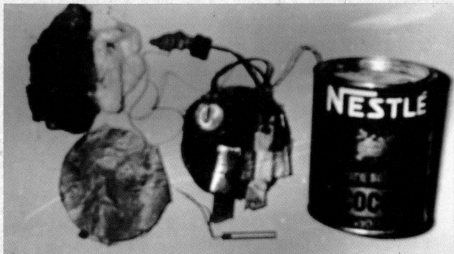

Main picture: South African troops mine-sweeping in Namibia.
Far left: The deployment of land-mines by SWAPO guerrillas has caused considerable trouble for the South Africans. By the late 1970s some roads in Namibia had to be swept daily.

Above: An ANC homemade bomb. During the early 1960s many of the ANC's bombs were of poor quality.
Left: South African troops checking a 'cuca' shop in Namibia. These shops provided provisions for guerrillas – some willingly, others unwillingly.

South African pressure, agreed in February 1984 to bar SWAPO from parts of southern Angola. Militarily SWAPO was unable to make the war prohibitive to the South African government; on the contrary, by the late 1970s SWAPO's losses were running at perhaps 1500 a year, as opposed to SADF losses of 50-60 per year, and PLAN activities had been confined mainly to Ovamboland. On the political front, however, SWAPO made considerable progress. According to many observers, SWAPO had gained the overwhelming support of the Ovambo tribe – whether for tribal or ideological reasons – and some support from non-Ovambos too. The possibility existed, therefore, that if Pretoria decided to accept an international settlement based upon free elections, SWAPO might well achieve a political victory at the ballot box.

If SWAPO found the South Africans a formidable foe so too did the Azanian nationalist movements – the African National Congress (ANC) which, together with the South African Communist Party (SACP), had formed a military wing called Umkhonto we Sizwe (Spear of the Nation), and the Pan-Africanist Congress (PAC), which had formed a military wing called Poqo. These movements were in many respects rivals rather than partners in that the ANC, a multiracial movement, sought a nonracial, democratic, socialist South Africa while the PAC, consisting of Africans only, wanted a system of government by and for Africans. However the two movements shared a basic common goal – the overthrow of the white-ruled *apartheid* state – and both had turned to violence in the early 1960s in an attempt to achieve their objectives. The ANC launched a sabotage campaign and the PAC a terrorist campaign within the South African Republic, but both campaigns were ineffectual and SAP managed to arrest or drive into exile nearly all the nationalist leaders.

The establishment of radical black regimes in Angola, Mozambique and Zimbabwe created new openings for the nationalists. Following the Soweto riots of 1976 thousands of young blacks fled the Republic, many to join PAC, which was training its forces in Libya and China, or the ANC/SACP, which used

Left: A UNITA guerrilla. It has been alleged that the SADF gave UNITA training, logistical and other support from the mid-1970s onwards, and that UNITA in return helped the South Africans in their campaign against SWAPO.

Right: South African policemen arresting black rioters in Soweto, June 1976. Thousands of young blacks fled South Africa during and after the Soweto riots, many to join the Azanian nationalist guerrilla movements.

Tanzania, Angola and Mozambique as its main training grounds. From the late 1970s onward, both of these movements, and the ANC/SACP in particular, began to infiltrate insurgents into the Republic, using Mozambique and to a lesser extent Swaziland, Lesotho and Botswana, as conduits. Targets included police stations, power lines, road and rail communications and state installations. Among the prestige targets hit were the SASOL fuel complex in June 1980, the Koeburg nuclear plant in December 1982, and the headquarters of the South African Air Force, in Pretoria, in May 1983.

Nevertheless, the Republic's 4,500,000 whites seemed resolved to fight for possession of a country that whites had lived in for over three centuries. Responding to the guerrilla threat, the government used its substantial economic wealth to build up a powerful military machine – with a

standing operational strength of 70,000 and a total mobilizable strength of 400,000 – capable of sustaining COIN campaigns against SWAPO and the ANC/SACP simultaneously. Pretoria used this military power – overwhelming in regional terms – to make its neighbors clamp down on the insurgent movements. Economic pressure was applied, cross-border raids launched against ANC offices and camps in Mozambique and Lesotho, and support was allegedly given to dissidents operating against the regimes of Samora Machel in Mozambique, Robert Mugabe in Zimbabwe and Lebua Jonathan in Lesotho. This policy of 'destabilization' worked, forcing the host states one by one to expel, or bar, the guerrillas. By 1984 the ANC/SACP had been forced, temporarily at least, to revert to internal sabotage.

If one of South Africa's main COIN methods has been that of supporting dissidents in neighboring states like

Mozambique, the existence of such groups illustrates an important point: that guerrilla warfare in Africa has not been the sole prerogative of those fighting against European colonialists or colonists. Certainly the major guerrilla campaigns in postwar Africa have been fought against colonial powers and/or white minority regimes, but numerous minor, and sometimes not so minor, campaigns have been waged by native African against native African. These include attempts to overthrow regimes, such as the guerrilla campaign waged by the Resistançia Nacional Moçambicana (RENAMO) in Mozambique (since 1975) and attempts to secede from existing states, such as the long campaign waged by various Eritrean nationalist movements since 1962 to break free from Ethiopia. It should not be assumed, therefore, that guerrilla warfare will decline because the decolonization of Africa has run its course.

The success of a
revolution: the banners fly in
Managua, Nicaragua, 1979.

4. LATIN AMERICA: THE MOVE TO THE CITIES

Historical events are invariably the product of a number of causes, but very occasionally an event or a sequence of events can be summarized by a single date or phrase that captures exactly its moment, the temper of its time, the nature of this set of circumstances. Urban Guerrilla warfare, a concept whose very name provides its own character reference, is such a phenomenon. It was the product not of a single cause but of many interrelated factors, and it was and remains a phenomenon inextricably linked with 1968 – the climacteric year of the Vietnam War and the year that saw the defeat of radical dissent by established authority throughout Western Europe and North America.

These two events, the Vietnam War and the failure of the European protest movements to change society in the manner in which the young demanded, were both causes and catalysts in the development of Urban guerrilla warfare, but if the latter can be said to have a home and a single cause that took precedence over all others then both are to be found in Latin America. Urban guerrilla warfare was a concept of revolutionary armed struggle that first found coherent expression in Latin America, and it was a form of insurgency that emerged from a Latin America that in the early and mid-1960s played unwilling host to a number of unsuccessful revolutionary campaigns. In the period 1961-67 revolutionaries throughout Central and South America sought to support and emulate the fledgling Cuban revolution by waging armed struggles. However, the revolutionaries' enthusiasm for and adherence to 'the lessons of the Cuban struggle' proved disastrously misplaced. The failure of 'the Cuban model' in Latin America in the period 1961-67 provided the incentive for a recasting of political and military ideas that was to lead various revolutionaries, in the period 1968-72, to the previously scorned concept of urban-based insurgency.

Cuba proved a false revolutionary dawn in Latin America in large part because Fidel Castro's successful campaign on the island between December 1956 and January 1959 was as misinter-

preted by revolutionaries after it was over as it was misunderstood at the time by its opponents. Castro and the Cuban leadership were partly responsible for this situation because they forced upon Latin American revolutionaries a partial view of the Cuban struggle that was represented as comprehensive and applicable to the continental mainland. To an audience only too willing to be convinced, Ernesto 'Che' Guevara in his

book *Guerrilla Warfare* provided a call to action and a 'Do-It-Yourself Guide' to would-be insurgents that was culled from the 'three fundamental lessons' of the Cuban war. These were that incumbent authority was not invincible and could be defeated by a people's war; that the countryside was the natural *modus operandi* for revolutionaries because insurgency was primarily a rural struggle concerned with the organization of

Above: An everyday occurrence in the later stages of Batista's rule: victims of the security force's often indiscriminate counterterrorism were usually left in streets and public places *pour encourager les autres.*
Above left: Batista's record between 1952-58 often obscures the fact that in the two previous decades he had commanded widespread support.
Top right: Batista: Running ever harder to stand in the same place.
Top: Along with canasta and horror films, cockfighting was Batista's favorite pastime.

rural society; that the revolutionaries, rather than awaiting favorable circumstances, could generate the momentum for their own success by direct action. Guevara turned his back on basic Leninist tactics and the concepts of Mao Tse-tung's protracted warfare, and set out conclusions for which good supporting evidence from the Cuban war appeared to be available but which were, by very narrow margins, erroneous. Uncritical acceptance of these conclusions compounded the revolutionaries' problems; a concept that in reality had never worked in Cuba had no chance of

success in the totally different conditions of the Latin American mainland.

The first of these theses – that revolutionaries could defeat the security forces – was the one that seemed the most obvious of the three and the one with which there could be no quarrel. Indeed, it appears so obvious and self-evident that it is all too easy to miss both its point and the reason why it proved so dubious a conclusion. Guevara's 'lesson' was a call to arms by assuring revolutionaries of the certainty of victory. Since the time that Latin America had won its independence from Portugal and Spain, the armed forces of the various states had enjoyed an aura of invincibility, and proven American willingness to intervene in defense of its interests and the status quo had merely confirmed this. Before Cuba the established order throughout Latin America seemed so secure that revolutionaries were unwilling to embark on militant courses of action that seemed doomed to fail. National armies in Latin America were strong and in most cases commanded widespread popular support. In caste-ridden societies they provided one of the very few means of social mobility, and the military's claims to be the arbiters of constitutions in the event of a breakdown of order, or corruption or incompetence on the part of governments were generally conceded in most countries –

Guerrilla campaigns in Central and South America

MEXICO

GUATEMALA
1962-81

MEXICO CITY

HAVANA

BELIZE
BELMOPAN

GUATEMALA CITY

SAN SALVADOR

HONDURAS

TEGUCIGALPA

EL SALVADOR
1968-85

NICARAGUA
1972-79

MANAGUA

SAN JOSE
COSTA RICA

PANAMA
CITY

PANAMA

U.S.A.

CUBA
1956-59

HAITI
DOMINICAN
REP.

PUERTO RICO

ATLANTIC

OCEAN

CARACAS

VENEZUELA
1960-68

BOGOTA

COLOMBIA
1964-68

QUITO

ECUADOR

GEORGETOWN

PARAMARIBO

CAYENNE
FRENCH GUIANA

GUYANA

SURINAM

PACIFIC

OCEAN

PERU
1961-65

LIMA

BRAZIL
1968-69

N

LA PAZ

BOLIVIA
1967

BRASILIA

PARAGUAY
1959-60

CHILE
1971-73

ASUNCION

SANTIAGO

ARGENTINA
1970-76

URUGUAY
1965-73

BUENOS AIRES

MONTEVIDEO

SOUTH ATLANTIC

OCEAN

FALKLAND IS.
(Brit.)

MERCATOR PROJECTION

Below: Photograph purporting to be the landings of Castro's guerrillas from the *Granma* on 2 December 1956 at Playa de los Colorados, near Belic, in Oriente province.
Map: Guerrilla activity in Latin America in the 1960s.
Below inset: Cuban revolutionaries photographed in the Sierra Maestra, 1957.

107

Left: Cuttings from Cuban newspapers detailing episodes and incidents in the 1956-58 campaign.
Right: The aftermath of the attack on the Moncada barracks that established Castro's reputation for daring and direct action, despite his failure and subsequent capture.
Below right: A symbol of Batista's regime: wives and mothers wait to visit political prisoners.
Below: Castro with fellow revolutionaries. Guevara is on the left.

as was the case when the Argentinian military ousted the civilian government in March 1976. Throughout Latin America, armies were one of the major pillars of the established order, and exercised such social and political power that their defeat and overthrow was inconceivable before Cuba. Castro's success destroyed this myth of invincibility, and this was the point of Guevara's first lesson.

The Cuban revolution may have shattered the myth of the invincibility of Latin American armies, but Guevara's 'first lesson' was simplistic and failed to take account of the very special circumstances that surrounded the Cuban Army with respect both to the place it occupied in national life and to its conduct of operations between 1956 and 1959. Unlike most Latin American armies, it enjoyed none of the prestige and authority that its counterparts on the mainland commanded. Cuba had not freed herself from Spanish rule but had been liberated by the Americans during

the war of 1898, and this fact, plus alternating American intervention in and direct rule over the island, demeaned the national army and denied it the status that other Latin American armies enjoyed by virtue of their being masters of their own households. The Cuban Army had no national niche, and it had little social standing because of its lack of a homogeneous officer corps that identified with a ruling-class interest.

In the 1950s the Cuban officer corps became heavily politicized, and polarized between supporters and opponents of the dictatorship of General Fulgencio Batista. This lack of unity within the

army and the army's lack of authority within society were crucial factors in its defeat in 1959. Promotion on the basis of political reliability rather than competence and an unenthusiastic rank and file combined to produce an army with a marked distaste for action. In the course of a two-year campaign the Cuban Army mobilized some 30,000 men, yet it lost only about 200 dead before it collapsed in a frantic *sauve qui peut*. For an army to disintegrate after incurring a less than one percent casualty rate in two years is proof that it owed its defeat to its own internal weaknesses, a lack of resolve and sheer unprofessionalism rather than

to enemy action. To misuse a phrase: the Cuban Army was not pushed but jumped. The army had no enthusiasm for the Batista regime, which dissipated whatever support it had among the population by indiscriminate counter-terrorism. Batista's only real basis of support among the military was from those elements whose past actions ensured that their lives were on the line in the event of failure.

Things were very different for revolutionaries in Latin America in the 1960s. Then the revolutionaries found themselves opposed by resolute and far more formidable armies, which, unlike the Cuban Army, did not give the revolutionaries a chance to recover from initial setbacks. In Cuba the army let Castro off the hook at the outset, and with the passing of time it became demoralized by its own failure. In the 1960s Latin American armies were on the alert, having been warned of the challenge they faced by Castro and Guevara, and they were better trained, better equipped and more determined than Batista's army had ever been. These considerations, plus the social support that these armies enjoyed, were vital in the defeat of rural insurgency in Latin America.

Guevara's second lesson, the alleged agrarian nature of revolutionary insurgency, again did not apply in mainland Latin America. A powerful if superficial case could be made to support the view that the Cuban Revolution was a rural struggle. Castro spent the entire campaign in the Sierra Maestra in eastern Cuba and no urban center of any significance fell to insurgent forces until the last days of the war when they advanced from the Sierra into central Cuba. But in formulating his second lesson, Guevara either never realized or deliberately refused to acknowledge the extent to which Castro's success depended on the support the insurgents had commanded from all sections of Cuban society, particularly from the towns. Castro claimed that the towns were 'the graveyard of revolutionaries and resources,' but they were crucial to his success. Towns had provided a constant stream of supporters forced from their homes by the feckless program of murder and torture unleashed by Batista as power

Below left: Attack on Moncada Garrison, Santiago de Cuba, led by Castro, 26 July 1953. It was an unsuccessful attempt to bring down Batista's regime.

Far left: In power for nearly 30 years, Castro remains a hero of the revolutionary Left. Seen here with Lieutenant Colonel Arnaido Tamayo Mendez (center), Cuba and Latin America's first astronaut.
Left: A Cuban military parade.
Below: The revolution remembered: the Plaza de la Revolucion in Havana today.

111

Above: Castro's triumph: 1 January 1959. Guevara is to the left.
Below left: Guevara in the sugar fields of Cuba, early 1960s.

slipped from his grasp. From the urban areas Castro drew the human, material and moral resources that brought him victory, while insurgent activity in the towns was crucial in dividing the security forces and ensuring their being off-balance and unable to devote their full attention to the campaign in the countryside. The often-missed truth about the Cuban campaign is that a largely unplanned combination of rural and urban insurgency brought Castro a victory that he could never have achieved had he tried to wage a campaign based solely on the peasantry of the Sierra. Indeed, Castro's attempt to wage a rural campaign *was* a failure for the first 18 months of the war, and it was not until the second half of 1958 – when Castro made a belated attempt to conduct a 'hearts and minds' policy in

Oriente province and when Batista's grip was failing throughout the island – that the insurgency had any real rural *and* revolutionary character.

For a variety of reasons the Guevara thesis, even if it had been accurate, could not have worked on the mainland in the 1960s. Throughout Latin America in general but the Andean states in particular, land and the question of agrarian reform were not explosive nor even major social and political issues. Flight from the countryside to the burgeoning cities was the principal reason for the pressure on the land never reaching crisis proportions, but also the South American Amerindians, some of whom still lived outside the cash economy, were probably the least suitable 'raw material' for social revolution anywhere in South America. Illiteracy, superstition, a traditional obedience to authority and wretchedly low levels of expectation dulled the impact of revolutionary appeals – particularly when those appeals were made by foreigners and directed against peasant boys who happened to be in uniform.

Above: Guevara in a heroic pose.
Top: Castro's entry into Havana,
January 1959.
Left: Three US Marines on patrol at
Guantanamo, US Naval Base in
Cuba, at the time of the Missile Crisis.
The base is still garrisoned today.

Above and right: The French radical writer Regis Debray (above), author of *Revolution In the Revolution* and collaborator of Guevara in Bolivia. His father, Maitre Georges Debray (right), at a press conference in 1968. The trial of Debray by the Bolivian authorities scandalized Western intellectual circles. Debray received 30 years, but was released early and returned to a comfortable existence in France.
Top left and left: La Paz, Bolivia, in the aftermath of one of the country's interminable coups, on this occasion the one that toppled President Paz Estenssoro in November 1964. Revolutionaries in the 1960s hoped to capitalize upon the discontent that produced such disorder.

Latin America was not inclined to revolution, least of all the countryside, and this fact was never more obvious than in Bolivia when Guevara made his disastrously incompetent and ultimately fatal attempt to raise the standard of revolt in 1967. After learning the main Indian dialect of Bolivia and then beginning operations in the one part of the country where it was not spoken, Guevara attempted to begin a rural insurgency campaign in one of the few Latin American countries to have undertaken a genuine land redistribution program and where the peasantry had more land than it could use effectively. In certain respects Bolivia was exceptional, but it and all Latin American states had a remarkably stable and compliant peasantry.

It was Guevara's third lesson, that revolutionaries could generate the conditions needed to ensure their own victory, that attracted most attention from the time that it was enunciated. Guevara believed that a small, mobile and hard-hitting group of professional and dedicated revolutionaries could, by successful armed action, produce the political and social crisis needed to ensure the collapse of established authority. Guevara argued that the *foco* (the insurrectional focus) could polarize society and guarantee revolutionary success. In arguing so elitist a view, Guevara overturned basic revolutionary orthodoxy.

Again, the Cuban revolution could be interpreted in such a manner as to confirm the validity of this idea, but this was a grotesque distortion of events. The truth of the Cuban revolution was that all the conditions for successful insurgency were present in Cuba even before Castro landed on the island in December 1956. Castro's very real achievement was to bring the disparate anti-Batista factions together under a single leadership and to take them to victory, and this was a very different process from *creating* a revolutionary movement and bringing it to victory by means of armed action. By the mid-1950s Cuban society was in the process of disintegration. Corruption, on a massive scale, together with the literal prostitution of the island and its resources to American business interests, had bred a total disenchantment with the Batista regime on the part of a cosmopolitan and sophisticated population. The island's large and powerful middle class was divided in its loyalties, but in the main it had little time for a general who had come to power through a coup rather than suffer ignominious defeat in a free election. The normal bastions of the established order, the church and military, were weak and all sections of society turned against a dictatorship that became ever more vicious as its position worsened.

Mainland Latin American societies in the 1960s were nothing like as volatile as Cuban society in the 1950s, quite the reverse. The passivity of the Amerindians – with one notable exception in Peru – was matched at all levels of society, nowhere more obviously than in the urban areas where the threats of unemployment and underemployment in a surplus labor market imposed caution on the workers. They, like many members of the professional middle class, were prisoners of the cost-of-living index, and they had little incentive to engage in activities that were not only dangerous but likely to leave their families destitute. Moreover, in the 1960s the very example of the Cuban revolution, through its Soviet connections, proved self-defeating. The polarization of society that revolutionaries sought took place, but it invariably operated against them because people regarded the choice confronting them not as one between liberty and reform on the one side and repression and the established order on the other. A choice between communism and the *status quo* resulted in a closing of ranks behind constituted authority, and even the local communist parties, because of their pro-Moscow orientation, eschewed direct action. They were the only organizations in society that might have provided the revolutionaries with the manpower and techniques needed to give them any chance of success and they were committed to constitutional action. The standing aside of the local communists from most of the revolutionary campaigns in Latin America in the 1960s was a major factor in the success of the security forces.

Moreover, the physical conditions of campaigning in Latin America were against the realization of the *foco* idea. Terrain and vegetation were favorable to the Cuban insurgents. The mountains were broken but not too difficult, and cover and targets were both freely available – as were sources of food and supplies for the insurgents. On the mainland conditions were very different. The jungle could give cover, but only at the cost of mobility, while the mountains and fast-flowing rivers often presented insurmountable obstacles to insurgents whose fieldcraft was generally poor. The Guevara expedition to Bolivia, for example, seems to have spent a good proportion of its time being lost, losing men drowned at river crossings and hacking a painstaking way through jungle – the very antithesis of a mobile, hard-hitting force. Throughout the Andes the paucity of communications and the ruggedness of the countryside aided the security forces because of their equipment, mobility and control of the air – advantages that the security forces enjoyed precisely because in the 1960s the United States committed itself to the maintenance of the *status quo*. Castro owed his success in part to the fact that American public opinion was divided over Cuba, the Eisenhower administration failing to recognize the unfolding pattern of defeat until it was too late to reverse it. Cuba burned American fingers very badly, and in its aftermath American resolve was never in any doubt. From the early 1960s onward the Americans embarked upon an increasingly forward policy in Latin America and the Caribbean, undertaking major aid and re-equipment programs, providing training facilities in various American military schools, and engaging in a number of covert activities. As the American involvement in Vietnam intensified, so did the American determination to stand firm in Latin America in order to forestall the nightmare of a war on two fronts. Such involvement proved sound, and it is worth noting that Guevara in Bolivia lasted less than two weeks after the Bolivian authorities deployed the last elements of their one and only (American-trained) Ranger battalion against him. American policy was a crucial factor in determining the fluctuating fortunes of the revolutionaries.

Such were the main features that determined revolutionary success in Cuba between 1956 and 1959 and failure on the mainland between 1959 and 1968. Obviously various local factors were at work in ensuring revolutionary defeats in the different parts of South and Central America, but as the surviving revolutionaries were forced to admit in the aftermath of failure, their defeats had been too emphatic and too consistent for there to be anything other than a general underlying cause to them. Failure in 'bubble campaigns' in 1959 and 1960 in Haiti, Nicaragua and Paraguay had been followed by more substantial defeats in Bolivia, Colombia, Guatemala, Peru and Venezuela, and in other instances revolutionary activity had been nipped in the bud by watchful security forces long before it had a chance to assume significant proportions. Defeated revolutionaries, forced back to the cities after their defeats throughout the Latin American countryside, were obliged to admit what

had become only too obvious: first, that the grip of the security forces on the countryside was too firm to be challenged at the present time; second, that even if the Guevara concept had worked in Cuba it was not immediately applicable to the mainland. Defeat forced the revolutionaries to do some thinking on their own behalf, to discard the doctrines that had been handed down to them from the Sierra Maestra, and the drift back to the towns was, of course, significant in its own right: it was an admittance that, if only for the moment, revolutionaries could not hope to survive except in an urban setting.

Of course, the failure of rural insurgency and the emergence of urban guerrilla warfare was not a simple and straightforward cause-and-effect affair; in part the two ran together and certain of the jigsaw pieces that went into the making of the idea of urban insurgency were in position long before the nadir of revolutionary endeavor was reached in Bolivia in 1967. The drift back to the

Below: A shanty home burns during the trouble in Bogota, Colombia, 1966. Left: The National Guard searches pedestrians, Panama City, July 1962.

117

towns on the part of defeated rural insurgents was arguably the most important single factor in the devising of the concept of urban guerrilla warfare, but one other urban factor weighed ever more heavily with revolutionaries as they began to analyse the causes of their past defeats. This was that insurgents were leaving behind Guevara's ideas of rural insurgency as Latin America became increasingly urban. In the mid-1960s Latin American populations became more than 50 percent urban, a state of affairs that had existed for many years in certain of the more sophisticated and important Latin American states such as Argentina, Chile, Uruguay and Venezuela. Increasing urbanization ensured that such countries as Brazil and Mexico joined the others in having more of its citizens in towns than in the rural areas, and revolutionaries began to realize not merely that rural guerrilla warfare was becoming ever more marginal to requirements given this growing concentration of power and people in the towns, but that a potentially explosive brew was being concocted. Latin American urbanization was not the result of industrialization, which was capital rather than labor intensive. Rather it was the result of the population explosion and the flight from the countryside, and in the aftermath of their rural defeats revolutionaries began to appreciate the pickings of unfulfilled expectation that might come their way on both counts. The cities of Latin America spawned 'misery-belts,' the shanty towns that were home to the unemployed, the drifters, the weak, the unfortunate and, above all, the young. By the mid-1960s two Latin Americans in five were under the age of 15 years, and in the anger of youth and the wretchedness of those who had nothing, revolutionaries anticipated a groundswell of support for their cause.

Thus Latin American revolutionaries came to see the cities as safe havens and as a potential source of support and recruits, but as time passed they realized that urban society was very vulnerable to disruption and that urban areas provided the means whereby armed struggle could be continued. For the first time obliged to look at the cities in terms of their operational potential, revolutionaries noted their concentration of high-value but virtually indefensible targets, the maze of access routes to and lines of withdrawal from those targets, the safe houses and publicity. Armed operations in the very heart of Western society were nothing if not highly photogenic, and they could not but have the maximum psychological impact upon the very people whom insurgents sought to impress. Herein lay the connection that crystalized at two distinct but inter-related levels between, on the one hand, those developments in town and country that had provided so much of the immediate impetus to the rise of urban guerrilla warfare, and, on the other, the various psychological factors that helped to account for this shift of revolutionary emphasis. Rural defeats and a return to the drawing board of insurgency coincided first, and at the lower level, with a period of considerable agitation and mass excitement in a Western society that was peculiarly impressionable at that time. It was the heyday of figures lionized at the time but now only dimly remembered across the years: Stokeley Carmichael, Eldridge Cleaver, Angela Davis, Abbie Hoffmann, Timothy Leary and Jerry Rubin are but six names that could be taken from fading newspaper headlines as a fairly representative sextet of 'the alternative society.' The 1960s marked the ascendancy of youth in the West.

Thus the recasting of insurgency concepts came at a time when American and Western European societies were receptive to dissent and fresh revolutionary ideas. In the course of the 1960s political philosophers from the New Left such as Herbert Marcuse taught the burgeoning student population of Western societies that it was the instrument of revolutionary change in an increasingly materialistic society. Marcuse, Reich, Adorno, Venegim and Debord were just some of the more influential writers who convinced a rising generation of radical students that the society in which they lived was as much an instrument of class oppression as it ever had been, and that society had

Top left: The 'misery-belt' – Chacarita slum in Ascuncion, Paraguay, 1959. Left: Rebel troops in Santiago, Chile, October 1969, when Eduardo Frei headed the government.

Above: Street demonstration led by trade unionist Clotario Blest Riffo against the Conservative Alessaniri government in Santiago, Chile 1960.

deliberately set about drawing the fangs of protest and change by presenting its members with a new set of worldly goods in the place of fervor, commitment and spiritual values. The New Left believed that the old Jewish concept that the individual was obliged to try to leave society better than he found it was dead, trampled to death in the stampede for consumer goods, automobiles and package holidays. Marcuse and others of similar persuasion believed that man in Western capitalist society was every bit as enslaved as his counterpart in the totalitarian societies of the Soviet bloc. Rejecting both Western capitalism and Soviet-styled communism, the New Left taught that established authority sought to control and manipulate individuals and to enforce their conformity, and that it did so by alienating man from everything that was real. By controlling environment, aspirations and consciousness, modern industrial society reduced men to cyphers and conditioned them into accepting an ordained role that 'accommodated' them within 'the system.' In a neat transposition of values that would have appealed to Nietzsche, Marcuse and the New Left were convinced that the most privileged elements within society were in reality the most oppressed, their very privilege and awareness of fortunate status being the instruments of guilt and enslavement.

Running through the New Left's concept of society was the view that the state maintained a dominant class interest through violence, sometimes mental and psychological and on other occasions physical. It was this institutionalized violence on the part of the state that, to the New Left, was justification for the use of violence against it, and herein lay the appeal and influence of one of the major cult-figures of the 1960s, Franz Fanon. A Martiniquais negro who died in 1961 from leukaemia, Fanon believed that society had to be changed and could only be changed through violence, and that violence was a personal cathartic – an individual could only find true expression and release in violence. To Fanon, violence was the means of social and individual cleansing. Violence was glamorous, and in the post-1967 world rugged good looks and violence came together in the ideal poster: Guevara. Heroic failure was more potent than success, but it was those who had failed and survived who were to develop urban guerrilla warfare.

Defeat proved a self-educating process to the rural insurgents in Latin America, and the newly enlightened were not slow to recognize the various developments that made for a change of revolutionary direction in the late 1960s. Their desire to continue their struggle, the new ideas of repression, violence and liberation, and a revival of the old anarchist belief in direct action as the means of changing society came together. Moreover, there was tangible proof of the photogenic qualities of violence and its politicizing effect upon society. 'The propaganda of the deed,' in the form of the Vietnam War, was imported into homes throughout the Western world by the television networks, and as a result American society divided and other Western countries showed splits that reflected this more serious polarization within the United States. Violence was seen to work, and as revolutionaries of many hues came to realize more clearly, urban violence had played a very considerable part in various revolutionary wars that had been fought since the end of World War II – and its track-record was not unimpressive. Palestine, the Suez Canal Zone, Cyprus, Algiers and Aden were all

Above: Insurgents in rural Venezuela, 1970. Despite the continued survival of such groups, Venezuela since Betancourt has enjoyed remarkable and unprecedented political stability. Top left: The high priest of the radical Left: Professor Herbert Marcuse. A refugee from Hitler's Germany, he saw the student movement as the instrument of revolutionary change.

examples of campaigns waged in whole or in part in urban areas, and where incumbent authority had been defeated. In Venezuela, too, a combination of rural action and an urban terrorist and propaganda campaign had been put into effect and for a time had seemed only too likely to succeed until in late 1963 a series of disastrous insurgent errors presented the initiative to the authorities

– and allowed President Romulo Betancourt to become the first democratically elected president in the history of Venezuela to complete a full term in office. Likewise, Guatemala had witnessed an attempt to develop an urban guerrilla campaign in the early 1960s, but this had been quickly and bloodily crushed by the government of Colonel Peralta Azurdia. Nevertheless, despite

the fact that two indigenous campaigns had failed in sharp contrast to campaigns that had been waged against colonial authorities, by 1968 the two organizations that were to be in the vanguard of urban guerrilla warfare had begun to emerge: the Acao Libertadora Nacional (ALN) in Brazil and the Movimiento de Liberacion Nacional (MLN) in neighboring Uruguay.

In the evolution of urban guerrilla warfare, Carlos Marighela's ALN and Raoul Sendic's MLN were to complement one another neatly, the former providing the theoretical treatise that quickly gained worldwide circulation while the latter provided practical example and inspiration. The MLN relied on practical experience, and its practice of urban guerrilla warfare was improvised. The ALN, on the other hand, proved too short-lived to be anything other than very theoretical and decidedly unfortunate, but its leader, Carlos Marighela, before his untimely death in the course of a Sao Paulo bank

Below left: Troops break up a student protest, Rio de Janeiro, Brazil, 1962.
Far left: Military police arrive to break up a 'pro-Cuba' rally, Rio de Janeiro, Brazil, 1962.
Left: Carlos Marighela, shot in a police ambush, November 1969, Sao Paulo, Brazil.
Below: Typical revolutionary 'wall art,' Montevideo, Uruguay, late 1960s.

raid in November 1969, published what was to become 'the bible' of urban insurgency. *The Minimanual of Urban Guerrilla Warfare* was to aspiring urban insurgents in the 1970s what Mao Tse-tung's *Protracted War* had been to earlier generations of rural revolutionaries, and for much the same reasons. Both provided a practical guide to military campaigning, and both set out in an easily understandable and coherent form the relationship between armed action and revolutionary strategy. Marighela's writings may have been marred by turgid polemics and may suffer in comparison with the more detached and measured observations of Abraham Guillen, the apologist of the MLN, but there was never any disputing their impact. Banned in such countries as France and with an immaculate pedigree provided by the author's 'martyrdom,' *The Minimanual of Urban Guerrilla Warfare* was paid the supreme compliment of imitation throughout the world, to the extent that the very word 'minimanual' was incorporated into various emulative

tracts, such as those prepared by the Official IRA.

The Minimanual of Urban Guerrilla Warfare has been a much-misunderstood thesis for some years. In part misunderstanding may have been induced by the very title, because *The Minimanual* was not concerned with urban guerrilla warfare *per se* but with the techniques of urban guerrilla warfare and the role it was to play in developing a wider revolutionary struggle in both town and country. Perhaps using Castro's campaign in Cuba as his model, Marighela set out a concept of warfare that embraced urban violence as the means of weakening the grip of the security forces throughout the Latin American countryside, preparatory to a revolutionary attempt to revive insurgency in rural areas. Marighela's concept of struggle was based on a fusion of rural and urban efforts, both being essential to revolutionary success since alone each would be destroyed by undivided security forces. Moreover, it was a concept that was more in tune with

Guevara's *foco* concept than is often realized. Tired of the Moscow-directed leadership of the Brazilian Communist Party that stressed that the route to power lay through legal and mass methods, Marighela embraced insurrectionary ideas that were every bit as elitist as those that Guevara had propounded and which were intended to achieve exactly the same result: the polarization of society and a consequent collapse of state power as a direct result of sustained violence on the part of a revolutionary minority.

The collapse of the moral authority and prestige of the state and the polarization of society were to be the achievements of the MLN in Uruguay after 1968 but, as this organization was to discover to its cost in 1973, there was to be as great and significant a difference between the collapse of the institutions of the state and the faltering of its moral authority as there was between dividing a society to the point where it was ungovernable and uniting society behind a popular revolutionary cause. Between 1968 and 1973 the MLN was to wage one of the most highly acclaimed of all urban guerrilla campaigns, but in the final analysis it was a campaign that failed because the MLN could not translate its undoubted success at one level – the destructive level – into the mass support that alone could have taken it to victory.

The MLN was one of the first insurgent groups to organize itself in the aftermath of the Cuban revolution, and it proved to be one of the most durable. It began life in 1962 or 1963 in the wake of an unsuccessful attempt to unionize the sugar workers of northern Uruguay. This failure prodded Sendic and his closest collaborators to the conclusion that rural effort was wasted in an increasingly urbanized society. In the case of the MLN, however, Uruguay was already one of the most urbanized societies in the world, with 80 percent of the population living in the towns and cities and one in two Uruguayans living in the capital. More pertinently, in the early 1960s Uruguay was already suffering from the various political, social and economic problems that have increasingly beset Western liberal democracies over the last two decades. Long one of

the most stable and prosperous of Latin American countries and one of the very few states south of the Rio Grande with more than a nodding acquaintanceship with democratic practice, Uruguay had developed an elaborate welfare system that a heavily padded economy could not sustain. With more than half the labor force employed by the state, Uruguay had a primary-producer economy that could no longer fund its welfare programs, maintain the high standards of living to which Uruguayans were accustomed and service a growing external debt. With inflation gathering pace and labor unrest growing, various sections of the constitution had to be suspended after 1965 as successive governments sought to stem mounting chaos by any means other than reform. With an entrenched two-party system that was incapable of dealing with the well-nigh insoluble problems confront-

ing the country, Uruguay in the middle and late 1960s was subjected to the process of social fragmentation that Marighela was to define as one of the aims of urban insurgency even before the MLN campaign began.

Though the first MLN operations took place in 1965, it was not until 1968 that its campaign began to get into its stride. Thereafter a series of audacious and often brilliantly planned and executed operations gave the MLN a marked tactical and psychological advantage over authorities that were humiliated by their all-too-obvious failure to maintain order and enforce the law. For some four years the MLN proceeded to give the Uruguayan government and security forces the runaround, its cell structure enabling it to withstand even the loss of Sendic and eight other members of the collective leadership in August 1970. In this period the MLN carried out a catalog of abductions, robberies, raids, jail-breaks and propaganda coups that ridiculed the government and exasperated a police force and army that was frustrated by their own failures and by the seeming irresolution of successive civilian governments.

But in 1971 two events were to show the limits of the effectiveness of the first generation urban guerrillas. First, in accordance with its belief that it had to wage a combined struggle in both town and country, the MLN tried to establish itself in rural areas – with all too predictable a result. Second, in November the presidential election resulted in a major defeat for the Left in general and, by implication, for the MLN in particular: for all its failures, the *blanco-colorado* party system commanded the support of the majority of the electorate. The failure of the MLN to broaden the base of both its military and political campaigns stemmed from a weakness which was partly structural and partly a 'character defect.' The MLN owed much of its success after 1968 to its method of organization. Compartmentalization into cells enabled the MLN to operate secretly with a high degree of security against infiltration and destruction. The same structure, however, made it all but impossible for the MLN to develop a mass organization that might have enabled it to capitalize upon its successes. The MLN had no means of channeling popular emotions into the revolutionary cause, and no coherent program for political change. In political terms the MLN was negative, both in its aims and its achievements. It was an opposition movement that associated itself with any number of 'popular' causes but with no clear idea of the type of society it hoped to create.

In the final analysis all that the MLN could and did achieve was the deepening of existing divisions within society to the point where Uruguay became ungovernable by democratic means. In so doing the MLN provoked an inevitable backlash on the part of the Right long before a hard-line conservative won the November 1971 presidential election, albeit on a minority vote. Anger at government failure to deal with the MLN in its infancy spawned a number of Right-

Above: Squatters in Buenos Aires, 1960.
Left: Uruguayan police crack down as the authorities respond to the kidnap of Geoffrey Jackson, 1971.
Top far left: Geoffrey Jackson, British envoy to Montevideo, kidnapped by the Tupamaros, January 1971.
Top left: Lucia Topolansky Saavedra, a Tupamaros activist arrested by Uruguayan security forces, 1971.

wing death squads as early as 1970, some of them enjoying the support and protection of certain members of the military who had no hesitation about infringing the prerogatives of the civil authorities and no scruples about the methods that should be employed against the MLN. The government increasingly depended on the military and military agencies enjoyed increasing success as they began to organize themselves effectively for the struggle with the MLN. By means of mass arrests, torture and outright murder the military had broken the MLN even by the time that the armed forces effectively stripped the president, congress and local authorities of their powers and privileges in the first half of 1973 and installed themselves as the rulers of the country.

One of the best-known and appropriate comments to be made about events in Uruguay between 1968 and 1973 was to the effect that the MLN guerrillas dug the grave of democracy and then pro-

ceeded to fall into it themselves. This was to be a fate they shared with two organizations across the Rio de la Plata in Argentina, the Montoneros and the Ejército Revolucionario del Pueblo (ERP), though there were crucial differences as well as similarities between the groups and campaigns in Uruguay and Argentina. Whereas the MLN was the product of a liberal and peaceful society that it set out to destroy, the Montoneros and ERP were the products and enemies of a faction-ridden society that in effect had been under military rule since the coup of September 1955 that had driven President Juan Peron Sosa into exile. Both had been formed in 1970 and were part of a Left that would have been hopelessly divided had it not been for a common hostility to the juntas that followed one another with monotonous and almost predictable regularity. Aware, however, of the deepening economic and financial crises facing the country and conscious of the unending hostility its rule provoked, the military relinquished its hold on power in 1973. By that stage, however, a pattern of violence as the means of bringing about change had been established, and it flourished rather than wilted under civilian rule. The brief and disastrous presidencies of first Peron (September 1973-July 1974) and then his widow Isabel (July 1974-March 1976) saw not only the Perons repudiate such Peronist movements as the Mon-

Left: Argentinian military junta, March 1976: Admiral Emilio Messera (left); General Orlando Agosti (right), General Jorge Videla (center).
Bottom left: Argentine troops armed with submachine guns outside Government House during a military coup against President Isabel Peron.
Below: President Leopoldo Galtieri at the height of his and the military's popularity in April 1982.

toneros on whose backs they had come back to power but their desertion of various radical causes that the Left had fondly believed a restored Peronist administration would put into effect. The result was that the various guerrilla groups of the Left, led by the Montoneros and Trotskyite ERP, set about the regime of Isabel Peron with all the ferocity of bitterly estranged bedfellows. Between July 1974 and March 1976 the scale of violence within Argentina rose sickeningly, with guerrilla groups and the security forces openly fighting not only on the streets of Buenos Aires but in helicopter-gunship battles over the capital. The country was all but in the grip of full-scale civil war by the time that the military decided that enough was enough and that the experiment in civilian rule had to be brought to an end. In March 1976 Señora Peron was eased from power (and thence into prison) by a popularly acclaimed coup led by General Jorge Videla.

Videla remained head of the military junta until 1981 when he handed over power to another general, Robert Viola, who was to last some nine months before being forced by his brother officers to cede the presidency to yet another general, Leopoldo Galtieri. In this period 'the process of national reorganization' manifestly failed to deal with Argentina's worsening social and economic problems, and the Falklands venture in April 1982 was partially mounted in an attempt to secure an international success that would divert public disaffection from the military's failure to deal with chronic domestic problems. More serious, however, was the fact that these failures in the economic and social fields were accompanied by repression on a scale and intensity that made anything that had happened under previous regimes or across the estuary in Uruguay look mild and amateur in comparison. Perhaps as many as 30,000 people perished at the hands of a military that after 1976 quite clearly believed that it would never have to give an account of its actions or face trial. In the short-term at least there was never any doubt about its effectiveness in putting down the various urban guerrilla groups of the Left, but leaving aside all questions of morality, whether such success was in the long-term interests of Argentina can hardly be said to be other than unproven by even the most inexacting of standards.

Indiscriminate counterterrorism was a feature of the Argentinian military's struggle against the Montoneros and ERP just as it was a feature of counterinsurgency campaigning in Brazil, El Salvador, Guatemala and Nicaragua. In Brazil counterterrorism proved very effective in dealing with a feeble, divided and demoralized opposition, but in the Central American republics it met with very mixed results. For a time Guatemala's civil war – which had rumbled along since 1954 when the Americans overthrew the democratically elected

Below: Yon Sosa, leader of the Guatemala MR-13 movement, seen (third from right) in the company of peasants.

127

Arbenz regime – seemed to have been brought to an end by the elimination of all possible sources of opposition to the incumbent junta, an estimated 20,000 people having been murdered by the security forces and associated death squads between 1966 and 1981. An upsurge in urban guerrilla activity, particularly in Guatemala City in 1981, served notice that the civil war was very far from over, and indeed by that time three major resistance movements had returned to the fray. The government's response, whether under Generals Lucas Garcia or Efrain Rios Montt, for the most part consisted of a continuation of indiscriminate repression, particularly in the countryside, seemingly to no very good effect other than to add to the number of dead. In neighboring El Salvador a similar pattern has prevailed, but in the aftermath of the recent elections the new center-right president, José Napoleón Duarte, has made overtures to the Frente Democrático Revolucionario/Frente Farabundo Marti para la Liberación Nacional (FDR/FMLN) opposition which may yet end a war that has claimed at least 30,000 civilian lives since 1979. In the case of El Salvador, however, much will depend upon the United States, which to date has tried – with varying degrees of success – to restrain the Right. In the event of a continuation of civil war the Duarte regime will face immense difficulties in using the security forces, which are noted for their lack of discipline, restraint and allegiance to the government against an enemy in control of perhaps 40 percent of the country.

Nicaragua, on the other hand, provides one example of counterterrorism proving self-defeating. The murder in 1978 of the leader of the opposition by members of the security forces was the single event that crystallized issues, triggered off a full-scale civil war, and provided a growing opposition with the unity and impetus it needed to sweep the incumbent Somoza regime aside. This opposition, the Frente Sandinista de Liberación Nacional (FSLN or Sandinistas), consisted of several groups, some of which had been in the field since the early 1960s, but it was not until the aftermath of the disastrous earthquakes of 1972 that the Sandinistas forces began

Bottom: Guerrillas in northern El Salvador, January 1981.
Right: Armed peasants in Nicaragua, 1982. Organized as a local militia, such people act as a significant boost to Sandinista strength.
Below right: Somoza's army in Managua, 1981.
Below: The moderate hope of El Salvador, 1982: President Jose Napoleon Duarte.

Above: Anastasio Somoza, president and virtual owner of Nicaragua.
Left: Sandinista troops under contra fire, northern Nicaragua, 1983.
Top: Nicaraguan children flee from a contra attack, June 1983.
Right: Nicaraguan rebel leader Pedro Joaquin Chamarros (center), with armed followers.

to assume significant proportions, the blatant and large-scale misappropriation of relief aid by the Somoza family and its acolytes being the *ne plus ultra*. By 1976 the FSLN had emerged as a force to be reckoned with, but it was to need over-reaction on the part of a family that had ruled Nicaragua as a dynastic fief for more than 40 years to produce the mass support needed to wage 'a combined struggle' successfully. The very speed of events in 1978 and 1979 and the totality with which a despicably corrupt and vicious regime fell apart have combined to disguise the fact that by June 1979 the FSLN had secured some 20 major cities and towns (including Managua) through a combination of urban violence and rural guerrilla warfare that had been in the making for some years. Amid the various arguments and tensions that have surrounded the Sandinista regime since July 1979 the significance of this fact has been largely ignored. Attention has been fixed upon the more obvious fact that by its very success and con-tinued existence, Nicaragua and its

Sandinista government is the vortex of disturbance in Central America, that they are to the 1980s what Cuba and Castro were to the 1960s. More signi-ficant, however, is the fact that between 1970 and 1980 the total urban popula-tion in the Third World grew by some 48 percent and that cities in the under-developed countries remain unable to absorb their population increase. Unable to sustain themselves by trade and industry, these cities have become ever more dependent upon their rural hinterland even as they concentrate poverty, disease, crime and unfulfilled expectation within their borders. It would seem somewhat unlikely that developed Western societies will suc-cumb to urban guerrillas, but if the example of Nicaragua is anything to go by, it is difficult to believe that rapidly urbanizing Third World countries will be anything other than peculiarly vul-nerable to a form of warfare that has been refined by setbacks and failures, but which remains, 15 years after Marighela's death, an unknown force.

Armed with a Soviet-supplied
Kalashnikov AK-47 assault rifle, an
Iraqi Marsh Arab stands guard against
Iranian attack, 1984.

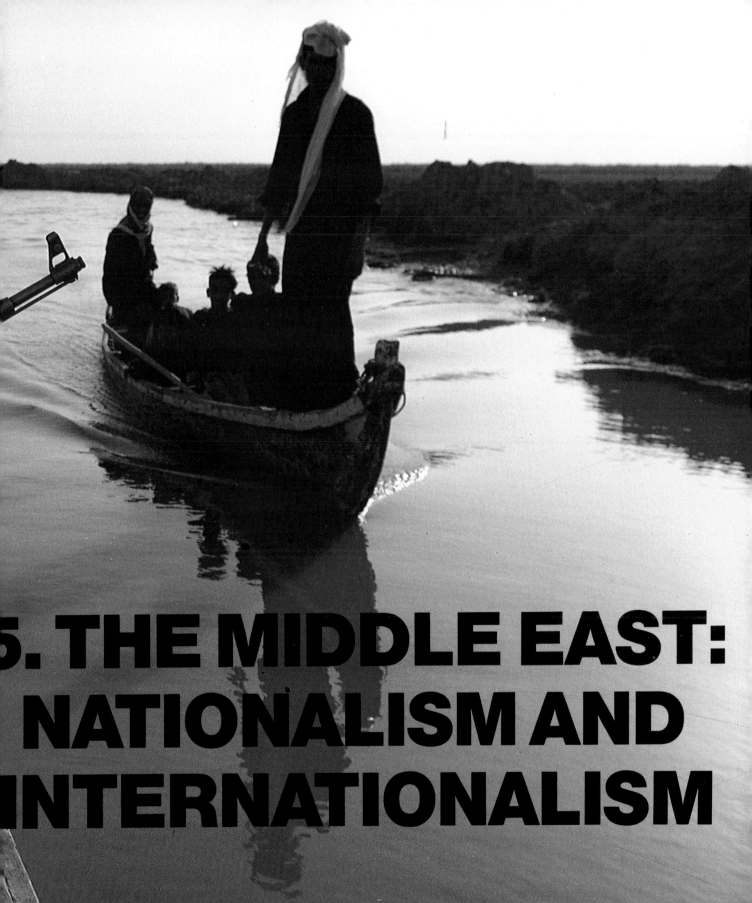

5. THE MIDDLE EAST: NATIONALISM AND INTERNATIONALISM

Defined as the combined territories of present-day Egypt, Israel, Jordan, Syria, Lebanon, Iraq, Iran, Saudi Arabia, North and South Yemen, Oman and the Gulf States, the Middle East has experienced more than its share of violence in modern times. Since the end of World War II, this has been manifested most dramatically in a series of military campaigns between the newly formed state of Israel and its Arab neighbors. By the early 1980s the world had witnessed six such campaigns: the Israeli 'War of Independence' of 1948-49; the Anglo-French-Israeli assault on Egypt in 1956; the Six Day War of June 1967; the so-called 'War of Attrition' between Israel and Egypt in 1969-70; the Yom Kippur War of October 1973; and the Israeli invasion of Lebanon in June 1982. Each campaign was more destructive than its predecessor and fought using the full range of foreign-supplied technology and weapons. When it is added that since September 1980 Iran

and Iraq, divided by religious as well as territorial differences, have been conducting a long and bitter war of attrition, it is tempting to regard the Middle East as a center for conventional military operations, contained only by the reluctance of the two main superpowers (the USA and USSR) to sanction further escalation.

But this would be to ignore a substrata of conflict in the region that has remained active throughout the post-1945 period, based upon lessons and experiences which date back far beyond the creation of Israel: that of guerrilla warfare. The region is well-suited to such campaigns. As Colonel T E Lawrence discovered in the Arabian peninsula during World War I, the indigenous tribesmen make ideal guerrilla fighters. Their close family and tribal links ensure the sort of coherence and discipline that guerrilla tactics require, while their intimate knowledge of seemingly inhospitable terrain and their ability to survive in climatic condi-

tions alien to most outsiders, gives them crucial advantages that may be exploited. Furthermore, the techniques of guerrilla warfare – hit-and-run raids by small, lightly armed mobile units, the isolation and destruction of enemy outposts, the interdiction of fixed lines of communication or supply – come naturally to nomadic peoples well versed in the subtleties of intertribal conflict. Admittedly, not all the people of the Middle East fit this pattern – a significant proportion are now city dwellers, far removed from the ties of tribal loyalty – but enough have existed and still do exist to make the creation of guerrilla bands a relatively straightforward task.

It would be wrong to imagine, however, that such bands only emerge when an outsider such as Lawrence appears, for there can be no doubt that in the Middle East, as elsewhere, guerrilla warfare can develop spontaneously, in response to a deeply felt grievance against indigenous or alien rulers. Between 1961 and 1975, for example,

A Kurdish guerrilla group, Pesh Merga, on parade near Mosul, Iraq, early 1970s. Most are armed with Soviet-supplied PPS submachine guns.

Above: Barzani, the Kurdish guerrilla leader, 1975, just before he went into exile after his revolt failed.
Above right: Iraqi soldiers guard surrendered Kurdish guerrillas, Zakho, northern Iraq, March 1975.

the Kurds – a collection of Aryan-Moslem tribes intent upon creating a national independent homeland in territory currently under the control of Iraq, Iran, Turkey, Syria and the USSR – fought a bitter guerrilla campaign, principally against the Iraquis in mountains to the east of Mosul. Under their leader, Mullah Mustafa Barzani, the Kurds began by exploiting their natural advantages of local knowledge and popular support to attack isolated Iraqi outposts and, when the Baghdad authorities responded by mounting large-scale conventional military sweeps into the contested area, gradually stepped up their actions against government forces tied to the roads and unfamiliar with the terrain. In the event, Barzani failed to win any long-term concessions (his movement virtually collapsed when Iranian support waned in 1975), but his followers did manage to inflict an estimated 60,000 casualties on the Iraqis. Nor has the revolt ceased to exist: although Barzani died in 1979, Kurdish tribes have taken full advantage of the disruption caused by the Iran-Iraq War to mount fresh attacks on both states.

A similar chain of events occurred in the Omani province of Dhofar between 1965 and 1975. Dissatisfaction with the rule of Sultan Said bin Taimur, coupled with a desire among the tribes of the Dhofar mountains (the 'jebel') for self-determination, led to the formation of the Dhofar Liberation Front and the beginning of guerrilla attacks on isolated outposts of the Sultan's Armed Forces (SAF) in the mid-1960s. By 1970 the guerrillas had gained the support of neighboring South Yemen – a development which led to an increase in Marxist influence and a change of name to the Popular Front for the Liberation of the Occupied Arabian Gulf (PFLOAG) – and had restricted the demoralized SAF to a few fortified posts and supply lines on the coastal plain around Salalah. These positions in turn came under sustained attack, and it was only with the overthrow of Said and the accession to power of his energetic son Qaboos in July 1970 that turned the tables. Qaboos, trained by the British, offered a tempting package of reforms and welfare benefits which gradually split the rebels from their supporters on the jebel, and made full use of seconded and contract British officers to mount a successful counterinsurgency campaign. Even then, it was not until the main PFLOAG supply line from South Yemen had been severed at Sarfait, that the guerrilla campaign began to falter.

Such campaigns have not always culminated in guerrilla defeat, as the existence of Marxist South Yemen bears witness. Formed in November 1967 from the British crown colony of Aden and a group of 20 emirates, sheikhdoms and sultanates known collectively since 1958 as the Federation of South Arabia, the state owes its independence in large measure to the actions of two main nationalist guerrilla groups – the National Liberation Front (NLF) and the Front for the Liberation of Occupied South Yemen (FLOSY). They operated principally in Aden itself, aiming not only to undermine British resolve and force a withdrawal but also to persuade the other members of the Federation that the guerrillas were the only contenders for post-independence political power. The campaign began in December 1963 with the attempted assassination of the High Commissioner, Sir Kennedy Trevaskis, and this incident was indicative of the guerrilla techniques to be employed over the next four years. Because the nationalists drew the bulk of their support from Aden, there was little opportunity to mount sustained operations in the rural hinterland (a tribal revolt in Radfan in 1963 had already been effectively contained by British and Federation troops), so the emphasis shifted to an urban campaign. Based in the rabbit-warren of huts in Crater (the market district of Aden) and Sheikh

Othman (an Arab settlement a few miles to the north of Aden Town), the guerrillas carried out a series of shootings, ambushes, hit-and-run attacks and bombings against the British and Federation authorities. However, the basic principles of unconventional warfare – the use of inaccessible areas (in this case urban slums) as sanctuary, the concentration of force against isolated, vulnerable targets, the dependence upon popular support – remained the same. In Aden, such principles led to success, for by late 1967, having suffered a steady toll of casualties, the British withdrew,

leaving the NLF and FLOSY to fight an inter-nationalist campaign (which the NLF won) to decide who should inherit political power.

Of course, it is possible to argue that the British, in the throes of economic crisis and desperate to save defense costs, withdrew from Aden because of domestic political problems rather than guerrilla pressure, but this does not alter the fact that the nationalists achieved their aims. This allows a comparison to be made with the campaigns in Kurdistan and Dhofar, out of which some basic lessons, applicable not just to

guerrilla groups of the Middle East, may emerge. The first concerns the need for strong domestic and external support. In all three campaigns, the guerrillas enjoyed the backing of people intent on achieving self-determination, but only in Aden was the appeal for outside aid answered by states (Egypt and North Yemen) capable of sustaining effective support. In Kurdistan the rebels enjoyed success against Iraq only so long as the Iranians remained firmly committed to their cause; in Dhofar the interdiction of the supply line from South Yemen spelled disaster for the PFLOAG. Simi-

Right: Sir Richard Turnball, High Commissioner of Aden (center, in dark glasses), discusses counterinsurgency tactics with British Army officers, February 1967. Despite their efforts, the Army was to be withdrawn by the end of the year.

Below right: Armed with the ubiquitous AK-47 assault rifle, a member of the NLF, face hidden, patrols the outskirts of Aden, 1967.

Below: Abdel Qawee Mackawee (right, in peaked cap), leader of FLOSY, urges his guerrillas to greater efforts during the war against the NLF.

larly, all three campaigns began from apparently unassailable bases in mountains or urban slums, but neither the Kurds nor the Dhofaris could maintain control of such areas in the long term. Finally, in both Kurdistan and Dhofar the government mounted effective campaigns against the guerrilla groups, either by swamping affected areas with overwhelming forces and firepower (as in Iraq) or by adopting proven methods of politico-military counterinsurgency (as in Dhofar). Only in Aden was the government response weakened by outside pressures, creating an atmosphere in which the guerrillas could flourish. All this suggests that to be successful, a guerrilla group must have widespread national and international support, an ability to mount attacks from the security of bases inaccessible to enemy forces, a willingness to adapt its techniques to local conditions and an element of luck.

It is with such a checklist in mind that a study may be made of what are undoubtedly the most important guerrilla groups of the Middle East since 1945 – those formed by the Jews in Palestine and, after the creation of the state of Israel in 1948, by the Palestinian Arabs in exile. The idea of establishing a Jewish 'homeland,' free from the pressures of European anti-Semitism, dates back to the late nineteenth century, when Theodor Herzl founded a politico-religious movement dedicated to a return of the Jews to their Biblical lands, in what was then still part of the Turkish province of Palestine. Known as Zionism, this movement enjoyed little official recognition until World War I led the Allied powers, desperate to gain the support of Jewish-Americans for an American declaration of war on Germany, to approach its leaders. At the same time Britain, already planning a future administration of Palestine under the terms of the Anglo-French Sykes-Picot Agreement of 1916, was not averse to the creation of a pro-European presence in the region, and it was from London that the most favorable response to Zionism emerged. On 2 November 1917, in the so-called Balfour Declaration, the British Foreign Secretary, Arthur Balfour, let it be known that his government viewed 'with favour

the establishment in Palestine of a national home for the Jewish people.'

Unfortunately this meant different things to different people. To the British it was little more than a wartime expedient which did nothing to sanction the creation of a separate Jewish state, and they therefore had no hesitation in restricting Jewish immigration once London had been granted a mandate over Palestine by the League of Nations in 1920. To the Jews, however, Balfour had seemed to promise the first step along the road to national self-determination, and they looked upon the restrictions as tantamount to betrayal. In the middle were the indigenous Arabs, convinced that it was all an Anglo-Jewish plot to take their land. It left the British in an invidious position, assailed from all quarters whatever their chosen policy. Increasingly during the interwar period, they faced armed opposition from both Jews and Arabs while also having to keep the two communities apart.

Jewish resistance groups began to emerge as early as 1920 when a local militia was set up, designed initially to protect *kibbutzim* (settlements) against Arab attack. Known as the Haganah (Defense), it consisted of ordinary men and women, trained in the rudimentary use of arms, who could be called out to defend their homes in an emergency, although it soon became apparent that this was not enough. As a result, in the late 1920s a special mobile element – the HISH – was formed, containing men of more advanced training who could act as a local 'fire brigade,' available to reinforce threatened Haganah groups. During the Arab Revolt of 1936-39 selected members of the HISH were trained (illegally) by the British officer Orde Wingate, who advocated a more active defense which included the mounting of pre-emptive hit-and-run raids on areas where Arabs were known to be preparing their attacks. Designated 'Special Night Squads,' they were the first Jewish groups to use guerrilla tactics. Their experience was to prove useful in the later campaign against the British, as was that of the Palmach (from *Plugoth Mahatz* or 'Shock Companies') of the Haganah, raised in 1941 as part of the defense of Palestine against the

growing Axis menace. By 1945 the Palmach and HISH together could muster over 10,000 activists, although their levels of armament and training tended to be low.

Neither the Haganah nor its off-shoots was a true guerrilla group, for although guerrilla techniques were occasionally adopted and all contributed to some extent to the anti-British campaign of the mid-1940s, they were closely controlled by their political masters in the Jewish Agency and widely regarded as forming the nucleus of a future conventional army. Such self-imposed restraint left the way clear for more extreme resistance groups, the most important and effective of which, created in the early 1930s, was the *Irgun Zvai Leumi* or ETZEL (usually known simply as the Irgun). By the beginning of World War II it had become the military arm of the radical New Zionist Organization, dedicated to the overthrow of British rule as a necessary preliminary to the creation of a Jewish state. Despite the emergence of the fascist threat, which caused many Jews to support Britain against the greater menace, the Irgun – led from 1942 by Menachem Begin – never ceased operations, hitting police and army posts in a campaign that culminated in November 1944 with the assassination of the British Minister for the Middle East, Lord Moyne. This action was condemned by the Jewish Agency, actively involved in negotiations with the British over the future of the mandate, and during the so-called 'Season' of late 1944/early 1945 elements of the Haganah hunted down the Irgun and its splinter group *Lohamei Heruth*

Above: Arab fighters, armed with a Bren light machine gun, service rifle and pistol defend Jerusalem, 1930s. Far left: Orde Wingate, the British officer who trained HISH units. Left: An Irgun member, armed with a Sten gun, outside a safe house, 1946. Below: Members of the Irgun practice with Stens and service rifles.

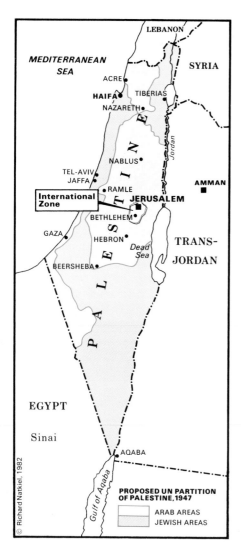

MEDITERRANEAN SEA

LEBANON

SYRIA

ACRE
HAIFA
NAZARETH
TIBERIAS

P A L E S T I N E

Jordan

NABLUS

TEL-AVIV
JAFFA

International Zone

RAMLE
JERUSALEM

AMMAN

BETHLEHEM

GAZA
HEBRON

Dead Sea

TRANS-JORDAN

BEERSHEBA

EGYPT

Sinai

AQABA

Gulf of Aqaba

© Richard Natkiel, 1982

PROPOSED UN PARTITION OF PALESTINE, 1947
ARAB AREAS
JEWISH AREAS

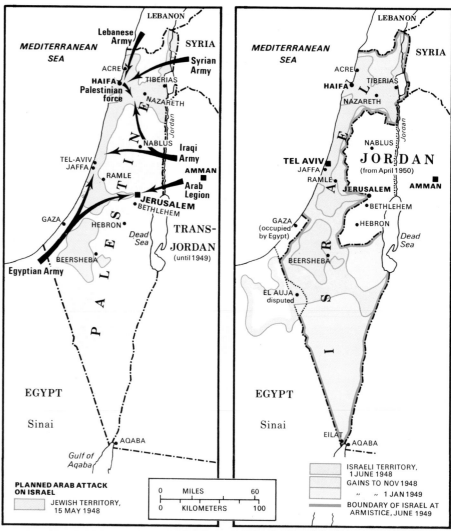

MEDITERRANEAN SEA

LEBANON

Lebanese Army

SYRIA

Syrian Army

ACRE
HAIFA
Palestinian force
NAZARETH

TIBERIAS

P A L E S T I N E

Jordan

NABLUS

Iraqi Army

TEL-AVIV
JAFFA

RAMLE

AMMAN

Arab Legion

JERUSALEM
BETHLEHEM

GAZA
HEBRON

Dead Sea

TRANS-JORDAN
(until 1949)

BEERSHEBA

Egyptian Army

EGYPT

Sinai

AQABA

Gulf of Aqaba

PLANNED ARAB ATTACK ON ISRAEL
JEWISH TERRITORY, 15 MAY 1948

0	MILES	60
0	KILOMETERS	100

MEDITERRANEAN SEA

LEBANON

SYRIA

ACRE
HAIFA
NAZARETH

TIBERIAS

I S R A E L

Jordan

NABLUS

JORDAN
(from April 1950)

TEL AVIV
JAFFA
RAMLE
JERUSALEM

AMMAN

BETHLEHEM

GAZA
(occupied by Egypt)
HEBRON

Dead Sea

BEERSHEBA

EL AUJA
disputed

EGYPT

Sinai

EILAT
AQABA

ISRAELI TERRITORY, 1 JUNE 1948
GAINS TO NOV 1948
" " 1 JAN 1949
BOUNDARY OF ISRAEL AT ARMISTICE, JUNE 1949

Israel (Fighters for the Freedom of Israel, known officially as LEHI but more popularly as the Stern Gang after its original leader, Avraham Stern). Captured guerrillas were imprisoned in remote *kibbutzim* or even handed over to the British.

The split in the Jewish camp did not last. By late 1945 it was apparent that Jewish Agency hopes for a relaxation of immigration controls to cater for the thousands of dispossessed survivors of the Holocaust in Europe were false, and in November the remnants of the Irgun and LEHI were rehabilitated, allying with the Haganah and Palmach to form the *Tenuat Hameri* (United Resistance Movement). A co-ordinated guerrilla campaign against the British began immediately, with Palmach attacks against police launches in Haifa harbor and Haganah sabotage of railroad targets. By December the Irgun and LEHI had joined in, hitting police and army buildings in Jerusalem, Jaffa and Tel

Jewish Agency found it virtually impossible to impose control over the Irgun and LEHI groups, many of which favored a campaign of terrorism to shock the British into withdrawal. Their attacks tended to be concentrated against people rather than property, eliciting a strong British response that included cordon-and-sweep operations in Jewish population areas. During one of these – Operation Agatha in late-June 1946 – large numbers of potentially incriminating documents were discovered and taken back to the King David Hotel in Jerusalem, headquarters of the British Secretariat in Palestine. On 22 July Irgun guerrillas, disguised as Arabs, planted seven milk-churn bombs in cellars beneath the British offices at the Hotel: when they exploded, 91 people

Top: A train derailed by Jewish guerrillas near Hadera, January 1946. Maps: (left) the UN Partition Plan, 1947; (center) the Arab attacks of 1948; (right) the outcome of the War of Independence, 1949.
Left: The King David Hotel blast, 22 July 1946; British soldiers and Palestine Police personnel help injured colleagues from the rubble.
Above: A boat, packed with Jewish refugees from Europe, approaches the coast, July 1946.

Aviv and killing 10 British service personnel. It was the beginning of a war which was to last until the British government formally announced its decision to relinquish the mandate to the United Nations and withdraw in 1948. By then terrorism had become the norm and 338 British civilians and military personnel had been killed.

The United Resistance Movement as such was not responsible for this success, having barely survived the first wave of attacks. From the start the

(Jews and Arabs as well as Britons) were killed. The Jewish Agency, appalled at the effects upon international opinion of such apparently indiscriminate terrorism, promptly withdrew its forces from the resistance campaign, leaving it firmly in the hands of more extremist groups.

By this time the Irgun could muster about 1500 active members while LEHI had less than 300, and it was perhaps inevitable that such small numbers should concentrate on terrorist operations to achieve maximum impact. Some guerrilla actions were carried out along traditional lines – on 30 March 1947, for example, the Shell Oil refinery at Haifa was bombed in an effort to destroy British economic investments in Palestine, and the railroad system suffered constant sabotage – but the main emphasis of the campaign shifted to direct attacks on members of the British Army and Palestine Police. Officers were assassinated, patrols attacked in the streets, roads mined and buildings bombed in a steadily increasing level of violence designed specifically to undermine the British government's resolve. At the same time, British countermeasures against captured and convicted terrorists were matched by retaliatory actions: in December 1946, for example, after two Irgun members had been sentenced to 18 strokes of the cane, a British major and three NCOs were abducted and flogged. This process of tit-for-tat culminated in July 1947, when in response to the execution of four convicted terrorists, two NCOs of the British Field Security Police, Clifford Martin and Mervyn Paice, were hanged by the Irgun and their booby-trapped bodies left in an orchard near Nathanya. In the face of such ruthlessness the British found it increasingly difficult to justify their continued presence in Palestine either at home or abroad and, as casualties mounted, the decision to withdraw must have been taken with some relief. The declaration of the state of Israel on 14 May 1948, 24 hours before the last of the British troops departed, was the outcome of a particularly successful guerrilla/terrorist campaign that was to act as a pattern for future groups intent upon the overthrow of a 'colonial' regime.

The reasons for this success may be analysed by reference to the checklist of guerrilla strengths previously outlined. To begin with, there can be no doubt that the anti-British activists enjoyed a wide measure of support from the Jewish population of Palestine, united in its desire for national self-determination and an end to the restrictions of British rule. Even the Jewish Agency, despite its official condemnation of specific acts of terrorism such as the King David Hotel blast, did little actively to prevent

Above: Women members of the Palmach prime hand grenades for use against the British, 1947.
Above left: The bodies of Sergeants Martin and Paice, executed by Jewish terrorists and left hanging in an orchard near Nethanya, July 1947.
Left: A British soldier steps round the body of a colleague, shot by a Jewish sniper.
Below: Two female members of the Stern Gang are escorted into court at Acre by Israeli civil police, October 1948. Terrorist groups had no place in the new Israeli state and were proscribed.

Irgun or LEHI operations. This near-unanimity of support gave the activists a natural base from which to mount their attacks, following the age-old guerrilla pattern of acting normally by day before emerging as fighters during the hours of darkness. At the same time, the Jews enjoyed significant international support, exploiting the feelings of collective guilt about the Holocaust in Europe and mobilizing American political and public opinion by means of an influential Jewish-American lobby. Indeed, the role of the United States was crucial, for not only did support for the Jewish cause put pressure on Britain, it also manifested itself in terms of money, arms and much-needed military equipment which, although donated privately by pro-Jewish groups, found its way to Palestine without official interference from Washington. Even the UN, dedicated to the pursuit of freedom and self-determination by peaceful means, did nothing to condemn or oppose the campaign, preferring to use its influence to smooth the way toward a British withdrawal and to sanction, through the partition of Palestine, the creation of an independent Jewish state.

All this would have been of little value if the resistance groups had not fought an effective campaign, geared to the realities of the situation facing them. Because of their small size and the concentration of Jewish settlements in precise areas of Palestine, a rural guerrilla campaign was unlikely to succeed, and although it may have been very difficult to justify morally, the adoption of terrorism, principally in the urban areas of Jerusalem, Jaffa and Tel Aviv, was appropriate. Such areas not only contained the best targets but also ones that, if destroyed, would have immediate impact upon British and world opinion. Attacks like that on the King David Hotel clearly contributed to an undermining of British resolve, giving the terrorists a distinct advantage in terms of morale and prestige as countermeasures against them failed to curtail activity. Britain had neither the means nor the will to fight for a mandate that no longer offered strategic advantages (especially after the independence of India in 1947) and to occupy a country against widespread international opposition. Admittedly, the Jews could take little credit for some of these factors (implying an element of luck on their side), but the fact that they were able to exploit British weaknesses showed that they had gauged the potential of their mixed guerrilla warfare/terrorism campaign to a fine degree. In this sense the victory of 1947-48, paving the way to the creation of an independent Israel, belonged in large measure to the resistance groups.

Guerrillas cannot defend a state, however, and as the Jews faced the need to consolidate and expand those areas earmarked for their control under the UN partition plan, the Haganah assumed importance. Between November 1947 and May 1948 it was gradually developed into a conventional army, capable of taking and holding land preparatory to its defense against attack from neighboring Arab powers. To begin with, the experience of the Irgun and LEHI could not be ignored, but the inappropriate methods of such groups soon became apparent, symbolized by the massacre of some 250 Arab civilians in the village of Deir Yassin, to the west of Jerusalem, on 9 April 1948. Conscious of the adverse effect upon world opinion of such actions, the Jewish Agency – already assuming the characteristics of state government – used the Haganah forcibly

to disarm and disband the guerrilla/terrorist organizations.

Even so, incidents such as Deir Yassin did contribute to the immediate security of Israel, forcing many Palestinian Arabs to flee from areas of Jewish control, which undoubtedly weakened their resistance to the formation of the new state. Thus, despite the existence of guerrilla groups under Palestinian control – notably around Jerusalem, where Abdel Kader el-Husseini led a force of about 5000 fighters, and Jaffa, where Hassan Salameh commanded a further 3000 – the response to Jewish expansion was weak, poorly co-ordinated and largely ineffective. A few raids were mounted against isolated Jewish settlements, roads were mined and military convoys ambushed, but compared to the growing threat of invasion by the large

conventional armies of Egypt, Transjordan, Iraq, Syria and Lebanon such low-level attacks were little more than pin-pricks, easily absorbed.

This established a pattern of Palestinian resistance that was to persist for over 15 years, during which time the Israelis were able to create and defend a viable state. In theory, the situation was ripe for the development of guerrilla warfare – people with an intimate knowledge of Israeli territory shared a common anger and sense of loss which guaranteed widespread support for military action – but for a number of reasons this did not materialize. With over 500,000 Palestinians in exile, occupying refugee camps in surrounding Arab states, it was impossible to co-ordinate a guerrilla response, and although small-scale attacks on Israel were organized,

Above: Palestinian women clean a Bren gun for their menfolk, members of the Jordanian National Guard, West Bank, 1952.

the *fedayeen* (freedom fighters) lacked both the means and the opportunity to develop into an independent force. Even if they had been able to do so, other problems emerged. Contact with the Palestinian population remaining in Israel – the essential 'safe base' from which to mount guerrilla attacks – was difficult in the face of strong Israeli policing, the Palestinian people as a whole were demoralized and, with the failure of Husseini and Salameh in 1948, their faith in guerrilla warfare was weak. The Palestinians had no choice but to depend on surrounding Arab powers, especially as those powers controlled key areas of pre-1948 Palestine – the Egyptians in the Gaza Strip and the Jordanians in Judea and Samaria (the 'West Bank') – and their nationalist dreams were quickly subordinated to the wider, initially attractive policies of pan-Arabism.

This was shown as early as 1951, when Palestinian exiles at the American University of Beirut, led by George Habash and Wadi Haddad, founded the Arab Nationalists' Movement (ANM), dedicated to 'eliminating Zionism and imperialism from the Arab world and creating a united Arab state embracing the Arab people from the Persian Gulf to the Atlantic Ocean.' It was a process that was to culminate in the formation of the Palestinian Liberation Organization (PLO) in May 1964. Sponsored and spawned by Arab powers rather than Palestinian nationalists, the PLO was an attempt to control and channel growing pressures from within the refugee camps for more positive action against Israel. Its military arm – the Palestine Liberation Army (PLA) – was to be geared toward conventional operations under the command of existing Arab armies and no provision was made for guerrilla operations.

The PLO could never satisfy the militant demands of the younger Palestinian refugees particularly when its leader, Ahmed al-Shukeiry, was clearly chosen by outside powers and could command neither respect nor support. A generation of Palestinians unaffected by the demoralization of 1948 was emerging, creating pressures which could not be answered by an Arab-sponsored 'front' organization. Instead they were beginning to turn to specifically Palestinian groups, dedicated to the principles of guerrilla warfare, of which the most influential was the Palestinian Liberation Movement, more commonly known as Fatah. It had its origins in Kuwait, where a number of exiled Palestinians, led by Yassir Arafat, Salah Khalaf, Khalal Wazir and Khaled al-Hassan, had come together in the late 1950s, free from the pressures of Arab frontline states. By 1964 they were preparing to carry out their first cross-border raids from the security of bases in Lebanon, spurred on by the knowledge that they were not the only nascent guerrilla group

Above: Ahmed al-Shukeiry, the first leader of the PLO, addresses a Palestinian crowd at Gaza, 1965.

among the refugees. At much the same time, in response to similar pressures, the ANM was forming the National Front for the Liberation of Palestine (NFLP), with its own military wing known as the 'Vengeance Youth.'

The first raids on Israel by these new groups occurred in December 1964. In purely military terms, they were insignificant – on 31 December, for example, Fatah carried out a raid on water pumps at el-Koton which the Israelis do not appear to have noticed – but in propaganda terms the effects were far-reaching. The Fatah communiqué of 1 January 1965 not only gave notice of the group's existence, but also promised to increase the scope and intensity of such raids in the future. Although there is little evidence to suggest that this new development alarmed Israel, the Arab powers saw their influence threatened. While Egypt and Jordan tried to defuse the situation by absorbing the guerrilla groups into the PLO, allowing them representation on the National Council and Executive Committee, the Syrians responded by forming their own Palestinian group, based on the revolutionary

Ba'ath Party. Known officially as the Vanguards of the Popular War of Liberation, but unofficially by the name of its military arm, as-Saiqa ('The Thunderbolt'), this was a relatively small organization, although it is interesting to note that it enjoyed (and still enjoys) the full backing of Damascus.

By 1965-66, therefore, the Arab powers had been forced to recognize a new mood of militancy among the Palestinians and had done their best to contain it, for fear of Israeli retaliation. To begin with, Fatah and the NFLP seem to have accepted this, believing in the final analysis that it was only through the deployment of regular Arab armies that Palestine could be liberated, but this changed dramatically in June 1967. During a war that lasted only six days, the armed forces of Egypt, Jordan and Syria were crushed by an Israeli blitzkrieg and vast areas of Arab territory – the Gaza Strip and Sinai, the West Bank and the Golan Heights – were lost. Henceforth, even if the Arabs rebuilt their forces, it was inevitable that their first priority would be the recovery of their own rather than Palestinian land. In short, after the Six Day War, the Palestinians were on their own.

The situation was further exacerbated by the fact that with the Arab defeat

Far left: The effects of the 1967 War on Palestinian resistance: Israeli soldiers capture Shukeiry's PLO propaganda office in Gaza, 7 June 1967.
Left: Paratroops of Gur's Brigade advance cautiously through the Old City of Jerusalem, June 1967. The fall of the city to the Jews was a major blow to Arab pride.
Right: The scale of Arab defeat, June 1967: an Egyptian convoy, caught by Israeli aircraft in the Mitla Pass.
Below: An Israeli machine-gun post overlooking the Sea of Galilee, 1967. The organization and professionalism of the Israeli Defense Force by the late 1960s made guerrilla infiltration difficult to effect.

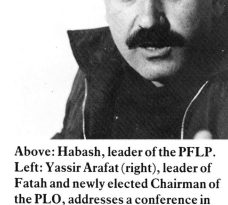

Above: Habash, leader of the PFLP. Left: Yassir Arafat (right), leader of Fatah and newly elected Chairman of the PLO, addresses a conference in Amman, 1969. His bodyguard is armed with an AK-47.

more and more refugees, including a massive influx from the new Israeli-controlled areas, looked to Fatah and the NFLP for leadership and hope. Arafat initially tried to exploit this by organizing resistance activities in the West Bank area. In late 1967 he travelled to Nablus to set up guerrilla groups deep behind Israeli lines and although this failed it did nothing to destroy his growing reputation as a dynamic leader. By this time he was in virtual control of Fatah and he used his new-found credibility – further enhanced on 21 March 1968 when an Israeli retaliatory raid on Karameh in Jordan was blunted by Palestinian defenders – to ensure the adoption of Fatah principles throughout the Palestinian movement. Basing his appeal simply upon the concept of the 'Return' – the liberation of Palestine from Israeli oppression – he gradually outmaneuvered the other guerrilla groups and by 1969 mounted a bid for power within the PLO. With the existing leadership discredited by their association with an Arab strategy that had failed in June 1967, Arafat faced a relatively easy task. In February 1969 he was elected Chairman of the ruling Executive Committee, assuming a position from which he could ensure Fatah domination and the adoption of guerrilla techniques, relatively free from interference by the Arab powers.

But this was only a first step, for the creation of a solid Fatah base within the refugee camps required an immense amount of work, particularly at grass-roots level. The process had already begun by 1969, with the establishment of Fatah propaganda and recruitment networks, and these were considerably enhanced once the full weight of the PLO could be brought to bear. Arafat ensured that all Intelligence and information was co-ordinated by a Central Information Council, and he used the PLO Research Center and the 'Voice of Palestine' broadcasting system, both formed in 1965, to disseminate the Fatah point of view. At the same time Fatah representatives, working under the auspices of the PLO, infiltrated deep into the refugee camps, enlisting support, rooting out potential opposition and recruiting future guerrillas. The aim was to create a Palestinian 'state-in-exile,' complete with its own central government (the PLO), army (the PLA), police force (the Palestinian Armed Struggle Command), education, justice and social welfare systems, which would be ready to take over in Palestine, with Arafat firmly at its head, as soon as Israel had been defeated. The guerrillas, meanwhile, would gradually undermine Israeli resolve and prepare the way for a Palestinian victory.

Unfortunately, Fatah had already

proved incapable of conducting an effective guerrilla campaign. Between 1965 and 1969 small groups of *fedayeen* tried to cross into Israel from bases in Jordan and Lebanon to attack isolated agricultural settlements, hoping thereby to destroy vital parts of the Israeli economy and demoralize the civilian population. Despite occasional successes – in February 1968, for example, fuel and water pipelines were destroyed near Nedt Hakikir, south of the Dead Sea – Israeli border security was too tight and the indigenous Arab population too subdued (particularly after June 1967) for the attacks to assume anything more than a nuisance value.

The effects elsewhere, however, were far-reaching, for as more militant Palestinian activists grew frustrated at the lack of Fatah success, they turned to radical philosophies in the search for an alternative approach. As early as November 1967 George Habash announced that the NFLP would amalgamate with two existing 'fringe' groups – the 'Heroes of the Return' and the Palestinian Liberation Front – to form the Popular Front for the Liberation of Palestine (PFLP), dedicated to a more active guerrilla campaign. Increasingly violent attacks against Israeli domestic targets were carried out; on 21 February 1969, for example, PFLP bombs killed two people and injured 20 in a crowded

merely copied his earlier tactic and founded new, more radical groups. In early 1969 Ahmed Jibril created the PFLP-General Command (PFLP-GC) and a few weeks later Naif Hawatmeh formed the Popular Democratic Front for the Liberation of Palestine (PDFLP). Both organizations had the specific intention of carrying out 'external operations' rather than cross-border raids into Israel itself. It was a campaign that was to come close to destroying the Palestinian movement altogether.

Left: The aftermath of the retaliatory Israeli action on Beirut Airport, 1968.
Bottom: Dawson's Field, 12 September 1970: the remains of the hijacked BOAC VC10.
Below: The Boeing 707 (left) and DC8 (right), blown up by the PFLP at Dawson's Field, 1970.

Jerusalem supermarket. However the new guerrillas experienced the same problems as Fatah and began to look for 'softer' targets beyond the reach of Israeli security. The campaign began on 22 July 1968, when three members of the PFLP hijacked an El Al Boeing 707 *en route* from Rome to Tel Aviv and demanded the release of 16 Palestinian prisoners in exchange for the passengers and crew. Caught by surprise, the Israelis gave in.

The Israelis were not slow to respond. Security on board all El Al aircraft was immediately tightened and official announcements made it clear that in future no prisoner exchanges would be sanctioned. Even so, the PFLP could hardly ignore its success and on 26 December 1968 terrorists struck again, this time at Athens airport, where grenades were thrown at an El Al airliner as it prepared for take-off. The Israelis retaliated in kind, sending commandos to Beirut two days later to take over the airport and destroy 13 Arab aircraft on the ground – an attack that threatened to drive a deep wedge between the Lebanese and the Palestinians. It also showed that Israeli targets were no longer viable, leading the terrorists to shift their attacks to the more vulnerable Western states which openly supported Israel. Habash may have argued against this development but he was outflanked by extremists who

The crisis began on 6 September 1970, when PFLP terrorists attempted a number of simultaneous plane hijacks. A TWA Boeing 707 and a Swissair DC8 aircraft were seized over Europe and flown to Dawson's Field, an ex-RAF airstrip in Jordan, while a third, a Pan Am Boeing 747, was diverted to Cairo and destroyed. A fourth attempt failed when security guards on board an El Al Boeing 707 shot one of the hijackers and captured his female accomplice, Leila Khaled, who was handed over to the British after an emergency landing at Heathrow. This led to yet another hijack three days later, when a BOAC VC 10 was seized and flown to Dawson's Field to join the other two airliners. All three were blown up on 12 September and a group of 58 hostages, held until various imprisoned terrorists were released by Britain, West Germany, Switzerland and Israel, disappeared into the refugee camps.

In the event, the European states acceded to the PFLP demands (Israel refused), but by then an unexpected development had occurred. On 17 September King Hussein, aware that the Dawson's Field incident threatened his authority as ruler of Jordan, committed his army to destroy the power of the Palestinians in his state. Despite a Syrian attempt to intervene, the Palestinians were defeated after heavy fighting and

pushed back into camps along the Jordan River. In July 1971 they were forced out of the country entirely; some fled to Syria but the majority moved to new camps in Lebanon – the only Arab front-line state that lacked the resolve to prevent such an influx – where Arafat faced the daunting task of rebuilding his shattered command structures and Fatah groups.

Hardly surprisingly, this led to a virtual cessation of guerrilla attacks into Israel for something like eight months, during which time the terrorists (whose capabilities were relatively unaffected) dominated the Palestinian movement. Under the new title 'Black September', they diverted much of their energy to attacks against Hussein. Their most spectacular success came on 28 November 1971 when they assassinated the Jordanian prime minister, Wasfi Tell, in Cairo. It was not until 1972 that Israel once more came under direct assault. By then the Palestinians had begun to forge links with other terrorist groups, offering money, arms and training facilities in exchange for involvement in operations against Israel, among the first of which occurred on 30 May 1972 when three members of the Japanese Red Army killed 28 people at Lod Airport. 'Black September' entered the fray on 5 September with the murder of 11 Israeli athletes at the Olympic Games in Munich.

**Above: Jubilation as the four Palestinians accused of assassinating Jordanian Prime Minister Wasfi Tell are released on bail, Cairo, 1972.
Above left: King Hussein of Jordan (in the lead), surveys the scene of a battle between his army and the PLO.**

Above right: Israeli Defense Minister Moshe Dayan (with eyepatch), arrives at Lod Airport in the aftermath of the terrorist attack 30 May 1972.
Below: Arafat (center) greets Erskine (left), the Ghanaian commander of UNIFIL, Beirut 1978.

Once again, the Israelis proved adept at retaliation; a special 'Wrath of God' assassination team was deployed to identify and kill all those responsible for the Munich attack. Of far more significance was the coolness that now seemed to develop between the Palestinians and their Arab front-line supporters. This was shown in October 1973 when Egypt, Jordan, Syria and Iraq initiated and fought a conventional war with Israel which did not directly involve the Palestinians. The aim of the war, moreover, was to recover territories lost in 1967, and although Egypt insisted on including the Palestinian question in subsequent peace talks, it was obvious that this was only of secondary importance.

Nevertheless, the idea of peace negotiations did suggest a new and potentially fruitful approach to the Palestinian problem and Arafat, aware that his policy of cross-border raids had not achieved success, now decided to alter his strategy to include a use of diplomacy. His aim appears to have been to isolate Israel on the world stage, thereby exerting pressure on Tel Aviv to reach a settlement, and in this he enjoyed remarkable short-term success. On 13 November 1974 he appeared before the General Assembly of the United Nations, receiving a welcome from the majority of delegates that was soon to be translated into more positive action.

Anti-Israeli resolutions were passed (the most famous, describing Zionism as 'a form of racism,' was adopted on 10 November 1975) and the PLO was accepted as the legitimate representative of the Palestinian people, enjoying 'observer status' on a wide range of UN committees. It was a major breakthrough, strengthening Arafat's position and ensuring his survival as Palestinian leader, regardless of his continued lack of military success.

Not all Palestinians supported this new move. As early as 10 October 1974 the PFLP, PFLP-GC, the Iraqi-backed Arab Liberation Front and the Palestine Popular Struggle Front joined forces in the so-called 'Rejection Front,' opposed to political compromise and dedicated to the defeat of Israel using purely military means. The PDFLP did not join them, but it was clear that Hawatmeh was of a similar opinion, having been involved in a series of terrorist attacks on Israeli civilian targets since the previous April, when 18 adults and children were killed at Kiryat Shmona. Similar attacks on Ma'alot (15 May) and Beit She'an (19 November) maintained the pressure, and although in each case Israeli security forces wiped out the PDFLP squads involved, each incident inevitably affected the morale of border settlements. If this had been combined with Arafat's diplomatic approach, Israel might have

been forced to consider concessions but, as had been so often the case, the Palestinians were hopelessly split into rival factions, with little chance of co-ordination.

The opportunity for concerted action soon passed. Continued American support for Israel undermined the effects of Arafat's UN 'victory' on the diplomatic front, while the 'Rejection Front' gradually lost its military effectiveness. As Western states responded to the threat of terrorism by improving aircraft security and forming specialist anti-terrorist forces, the normal forms of attack – plane hijacks, kidnaps and assassinations – became more difficult. Some successes were still achieved. On 21 December 1975, for example, six members of the Arm of the Arab Revolution (a cover term for the PFLP), led by the Venezuelan terrorist Ilich Ramirez Sanchez ('Carlos'), kidnapped eleven oil ministers attending the Organization of Petroleum Exporting Countries (OPEC) meeting in Vienna; but such successes became progressively fewer. With the Israeli rescue mission to Entebbe (Uganda) on 3/4 July 1976, mounted in response to the hijack of an Air France

airliner by a combined Baader-Meinhof/ PFLP group, this particular terrorist tactic lost much of its appeal. When the West Germans mounted a similar mission to Mogadishu (Somalia) in October 1977 to rescue the passengers and crew of a Lufthansa Boeing 737, hijacked by a previously unknown Palestinian group (the Organization of Struggle against World Imperialism), plane hijacks virtually ceased.

Such a terrorist failure should have allowed Arafat, as the only Palestinian leader retaining credibility among the refugees, to reassert PLO control of the resistance movement, but this he was unable to do. Since 1970-71 he had been steadily reorganizing the Fatah networks in Lebanon, achieving some success in 1973 when he established the right of the PLO to defend the refugee camps, but as the situation in Lebanon degenerated into civil war the Palestinians were drawn inexorably into the politics of their host state, dissipating their energies on campaigns in support of the Moslem factions against the ruling Maronite Christian elite. By 1976, with the Syrians rather paradoxically supporting the Christians and the Pales-

tinians forced to retreat to camps in the south of Lebanon, all pretense at Arab unity had disappeared and the PLO had been undeniably weakened. The emergence of a new terrorist organization, 'Black June,' led by Abu Nidal, did nothing to improve matters, wasting its efforts against Syrian rather than Israeli targets. The resistance movement was by now fragmented and in a particularly poor state.

Nevertheless, between 1976 and 1982 the PLO did begin to recover. Its concentration in the camps of southern Lebanon enabled Arafat to assert a degree of local control and, as Fatah strength slowly increased, a series of artillery and rocket attacks were made on Israeli settlements in northern Galilee, coinciding with renewed PDFLP bombings in Israel itself. In response the Israelis mounted a number of cross-border retaliatory raids. The most ambitious raid was Operation Litani in March 1978, which threatened to destroy the Palestinian camps. But the PLO was prepared; they withdrew northward, drawing the Israelis deep into Lebanon and into a commitment they could not afford. As the IDF pulled

back, having achieved very little of lasting value, Arafat's credibility improved dramatically. When the Camp David Agreement between Egypt and Israel six months later sounded the death-knell for the 'Rejection Front' (irrelevant at a time when diplomacy was clearly achieving results, even if those results were opposed by the majority of Palestinians) the splinter groups re-entered the PLO framework, accepting a Fatah call for the establishment, through political as well as military action, of an independent Palestinian homeland.

This was an extremely worrying development for the Israelis to contemplate and, as cross-border bombardments by the PLO continued, it became obvious that the Palestinian movement was revitalized and capable of imposing damage, at least to the Galilee settlements. By the end of 1978 UN troops had been deployed between the refugee camps and northern Israel, but their effects were minimal and, when Palestinian 'external operations' restarted, with a spate of assassinations in various West European cities, the Israelis felt forced to act. On 4 June 1982, in response to the attempted assassination of Israeli ambassador Shlomo Argov in London, Israeli jets attacked refugee camps in southern Lebanon and, two days later, in Operation Peace for Galilee, armored forces advanced northward through UN lines.

Initially the Israelis spoke of a limited incursion only, designed to push the PLO back until its guns were out of range of Galilee, but it was soon

apparent that something much more elaborate was being effected, namely the destruction of the PLO. Seaborne landings at Sidon and Damour trapped many of the Palestinian fighters before they could repeat the tactic of 1978 and withdraw northward, the outskirts of Beirut were entered and, inland, the Syrian threat in the Beqa'a Valley was contained, principally by means of highly accurate air strikes on surface-to-air missile (SAM) sites. With the Christian government in Beirut doing nothing to prevent the Israeli advance and Syria apparently deterred from entering the battle, the PLO was soon isolated, with its back to the sea, in West Beirut. Arafat had little choice but to accept a US plan for evacuation. In late August 1982 the bulk of the Palestinian fighters, an estimated 14,000 men, left Lebanon under the eyes of a special multinational force of US, French and Italian troops, in a third and much more decisive departure, this time to places as far afield as Tunisia, South Yemen and Iraq. With no other sanctuary close to Israel now available it was a potentially mortal blow.

Since that time Arafat has continued to enjoy political status – he is still seen by many states as the only real representative of the Palestinian people – but militarily he has been destroyed. Not only the Fatah groups departed with him but also the remnants of the PFLP, PDFLP (now renamed the Democratic Front for the Liberation of Palestine – DFLP) and PFLP-GC, as well as a substantial proportion of the PLA. They are now in exile far from Israel and

Above: A member of Abu Nidal's 'Black June' movement, arrested by Italian police after an occupation of the Syrian Embassy in Rome, 1976.
Above left: Israeli troops lead blindfold Egyptian prisoners towards their lines, 20 October 1973.
Below right: Israeli General Avigdor Ben Gal (left) greets a local Phalangist militia leader at Mis e-Jebel in Lebanon during the abortive Operation Litani, March 1978.
Below: A young Palestinian commando, Hamid Nadim, in Israeli captivity after coming ashore to attack Israeli settlements, 1977.

Below: An IDF camp, south of the Beirut-Damascus road, Operation Peace for Galilee, June 1982. A 155mm M109A1 self-propelled artillery piece is in the foreground.

Right: A Lebanese Phalange militiaman, with Israeli soldier for company, mans a vehicle checkpoint on the line dividing East (Christian) and West (Moslem) Beirut, August 1982.

Bottom right: Israeli soldiers advance warily into West Beirut, September 1982. Street fighting against seasoned guerrillas proved to be a problem. Bottom left: Israeli forces stand guard over captured Palestinian and Moslem militia arms, Sidon, June 1982.

although there is evidence that some fighters (including Arafat himself) have tried to drift back into the continued chaos of Lebanon, they have found their way blocked, not just by the Israelis and Maronites but, more significantly, by Syria. In late 1983 a virtual Palestinian civil war was fought around Tripoli in northern Lebanon, in which one of the last Fatah enclaves were squeezed out by Abu Musa and his Syrian-backed forces in what can only be seen as a Syrian move to exert control over the Palestinian cause. If this is so, the guerrilla war may not yet be ended – the prospects were worrying enough for the Israelis to remain in the southern Lebanese buffer zone until early 1985, regardless of the human and economic drain such a commitment entailed. However by that time the Palestinian guerrilla threat, together with its terrorist offshoot, had declined. A few hit-and-run raids on Israel itself by small squads of terrorists continued to be reported, but their impact was no stronger than that of their predecessors 20 years earlier.

The Palestinian guerrillas have therefore enjoyed little lasting success, and the reasons are not difficult to discern. Despite a widespread desire among the refugees for self-determination and a return to Palestine, the PLO/Fatah leadership has never been able to ensure complete support for its policies, having to accept throughout its history the existence of a plethora of rival guerrilla and terrorist groups, each of which dissipated resources and diluted fighting potential, often to the extent of leaving Israel free from any form of attack. At the same time, the Palestinians as a whole never enjoyed the advantages of secure bases from which to mount their attacks, lacking any infrastructure within Israel or the occupied territories and progressively alienating surrounding Arab states. Once Jordan had forced the refugees to move elsewhere in 1970-71, Lebanon was the only alternative location contiguous with Israel, and the war of June-September 1982 put paid to that. The continued presence of Syrian-backed PLO, PLA and Saiqa groups in Lebanon may produce a renewed guerrilla campaign in the future, but it is unlikely to be carried out for purely Palestinian gains. Even if it does

Above left: Israeli troops man positions overlooking the Palestinian camp at Bourj el-Barajneh, 1982. Below far left: Israeli and Lebanese soldiers on a well-armed M113 APC are welcomed by Arab women on the road to Beirut, 1982.

Above: A young Palestinian fighter, armed with a Soviet-made RFG-7 anti-tank rocket, trains in northern Lebanon, 1984. Below left: Palestinians suspected of guerrilla activities are rounded up for interrogation by the IDF, June 1982.

materialize, the record of Israel retaliation, both to local cross-border guerrilla raids and to terrorist attacks on the wider international scene, suggests that it will have enormous problems even approaching its targets, while the morale of the Palestinian refugees, particularly since the defeat of the PLO in Beirut and the horrific massacres at Sabra and Chatilla in 1982, is not high enough to guarantee support for future military action. This may, of course, be nothing more than a trough in the fortunes of the Palestinian people who after all still command a high degree of political respect worldwide. Diplomatic efforts continue to be made, through Arafat as Chairman of the PLO, to gain a peaceful settlement but there can be no denying that, as a guerrilla organization, the Palestinians have not enjoyed a great deal of success.

I.R.A
GRAMER
DANNY
DAN

TONY
PEA
Up. The Punks
SEXPISTOLS

SHANDO
ARDER
TOTES
MONTY

JW KEVY
JOELLISKY Dano
WALDO MURPH
MUSSER

6. EUROPE: THE USE OF TERROR

An officer of the Royal Ulster
Constabulary on patrol in the city
center, Belfast.

Terrorism is the commitment of acts of extreme violence or intimidation for political ends. Its motives are sometimes ideological and philosophical and sometimes nationalist. In Europe, for example, a nationalist-inspired assassination sparked off World War I. On 28 June 1914 at Sarajevo, Gavrilo Princip, a nineteen-year-old student who belonged to the secret terrorist society the 'Black Hand,' shot and killed the Archduke Franz Ferdinand, heir to the Austrian throne, hoping thereby to further the cause of Serbian independence. Isolated acts of terrorism of this sort have undoubtedly affected the course of history, but in more recent times it is the growth of systematic terrorist campaigns that has challenged European governments.

The willingness to use violence in this way has traditionally produced campaigns of guerrilla warfare, as seen in Greece during the years 1946 to 1949. As a result of the German invasion of Greece in 1941, resistance groups sprang up in the countryside and especially in the mountains. Some were rooted in Left-wing ideological inspiration and others to the center or right and all had different ideas about the future of Greece once liberation had been achieved. As a result, the Democratic Army of Greece (DSE), backed by the Soviet Union, found itself at odds with the Greek National Army (GNA), supported by the British and later the Americans, and the right-wing former resistance movements. This led to a guerrilla campaign which lasted three years, during which the DSE adopted classic guerrilla tactics of retreating to the safety of the mountains and avoiding head-on clashes with the better equipped GNA, while laying mines and setting booby-traps. The DSE survived for so long because its members could resort to the bordering communist countries of Albania, Yugoslavia and Bulgaria for sanctuary. This provided them with the opportunity to train, regroup and rearm and then to return to the fray in the mountains of Macedonia and Thessaly, especially the Grammos and Vitsi ranges. But as the DSE grew larger it lost its guerrilla advantages and was organized into military-style battalions and brigades. It was then tempted

into larger confrontations with the GNA and lost out to the GNA's superior firepower. In addition, the split between Tito of Yugoslavia and Stalin of the Soviet Union led to the closure of the former's border with Greece, and when Albania and Bulgaria followed suit, the DSE was unable to continue operations. The end of this campaign was, therefore, sudden and complete, with an estimated death-toll of 50,000, and this led many to query the efficacy of guerrilla warfare within relatively sophisticated Europe.

Yet only a few years later the Greeks were involved in another guerrilla war – on Cyprus. British possession of the island was brought into question by the growth of a Greek-Cypriot nationalist movement led by Archbishop Makarios. Greek Cypriots, who made up three-quarters of the population of Cyprus,

**Above: British troops search for
EOKA suspects, Nicosia, Cyprus.
Above left: Two partisans of the DSE
stand guard in World War II.
Left: Nikitos, a DSE guerrilla
commander in Northern Greece.
Right: A British car ambushed by
EOKA guerrillas.**

aimed to unify Greece and Cyprus after
British withdrawal, a policy known as
enosis, but the Turkish-Cypriot community were vehemently opposed to the
idea. British proposals for withdrawal
were found to be unsatisfactory in 1954
and the extremist element of the Greek
Cypriots formed the National Organization of Cypriot Fighters (EOKA) under
George Grivas in order to use military
force to persuade Britain to leave. For
four years, from 1955 to 1959, Grivas led

a guerrilla war against the British presence, having set EOKA up as a national liberation movement.

EOKA guerrillas operated in the towns at first but gradually moved to the security of the Troodos Mountains where Grivas set up his main headquarters. He then organized regional headquarters, sector headquarters and local commanders, with mountain groups responsible for rural raids and ambushes and town groups responsible for sabotage, shooting and bombing. Most of the military activity of EOKA was aimed at British forces and installations, using hit-and-run tactics against isolated police posts or British patrols. In this way a few hundred insurgents were able to take on 25,000 British troops, who had only limited success in trying to counter such activity. They resorted to arrests, detentions, internment, curfews and deportation to try to end the campaign, but EOKA, which never aimed at complete military victory over the British, were successful in making it very expensive for Britain to stay. At the end of 1958 a ceasefire was arranged so that negotiations between all interested parties could take place to end the conflict. The Greek Cypriots still favored *enosis*, and were afraid that the Turks favored partition, while the British were in between; eventually independence was found to be an

acceptable compromise. Once again, the use of guerrilla tactics had not produced the desired result and it is interesting to note that Grivas had, on a number of occasions, resorted to rudimentary terrorism to force his way through the ensuing stalemate. It was a development that was to be remembered, particularly when other groups took the same course elsewhere.

Britain had problems in Ireland at the same time. The question of Irish independence had been raised in the early part of the century but complex historical, religious and economic factors made it a contentious issue. The creation of an independent Southern Ireland consisting of 26 counties alongside Ulster (Northern Ireland) consisting of six counties to remain part of the United Kingdom, seemed to be the best chance for success that existed in 1920-22. The Irish campaign for independence, however, led to the creation of a military wing of the Irish nationalist movement, known as the Irish Republican Army (IRA), which refused to accept the division of Ireland. A united Ireland has been the aim of the IRA ever since. It has mounted major campaigns just prior to World War II, in the 1950s and from 1969 to the present day.

IRA strategy in the mid-1950s was designed to force the British to abandon Ulster, leaving the road open to reunification. The tactic was to use flying columns of armed republicans, which attacked police barracks, customs posts and army centers around the border area. The IRA's planning and organization at the time was poor, and members from Southern Ireland were operating in unfamiliar territory with a fairly apathetic Catholic local population and a very actively hostile Unionist one. Army barracks were a favorite target, especially if they yielded arms for the organization, but there were also incidents involving the burning of buses, bombings, killings and booby-traps along with isolated incidents in England. In response internment was introduced and the Royal Ulster Constabulary (RUC), backed up by the British Army, concentrated upon patrolling, setting up road blocks and instituting house searches. In the South, too, the government tightened security, perceiving the

Above: French philosopher Jean Paul Sartre addresses students at the Sorbonne, Paris, May 1968. The students had occupied the building. Far left: Grivas, leader of EOKA.

IRA's campaign to be a threat to stability in all Ireland, with the result that many IRA activists found themselves in prison in Southern Ireland. The number of incidents began to fall off in 1958, but the campaign was not halted until the beginning of 1962. Over 600 incidents had taken place, with 15 people dead and many others injured or in jail, and a 'mix' of guerrilla and terrorist techniques had begun to emerge. They were to be repeated at the end of the decade.

Thus, for the first 20 years after World War II, Europe encountered sporadic outbreaks of guerrilla warfare with terrorist tactics as a developing trend. It is important to stress, however, that such campaigns were limited to Western Europe, since Eastern Europe had been occupied by Soviet forces in 1945 and the Soviet Union had ensured that communist regimes took over within four years. The presence of Soviet armed forces and the authoritarian nature of those regimes has prevented guerrilla warfare from infiltrating Eastern Europe to any sustained degree. Indeed, conventional military force has always been preferred, having been used by the

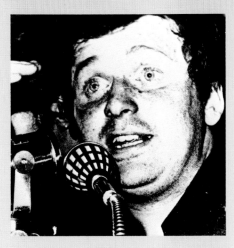

Soviet Union to intervene directly in the
internal affairs of Hungary in 1956 and
in Czechoslovakia in 1968. This con-
trasts sharply to the situation in Western
Europe, which was confronted in the
late 1960s by student rebellions that
were to give rise to a wave of terrorist
activity across the continent. The popu-
larization of terrorism led groups in
Ireland, Spain and the Netherlands to
use similar techniques, and the problem
was further compounded by non--
European groups using terrorism as a
political weapon inside Europe. The
1970s saw a complicated web of diverse
groups resorting to terrorism for different reasons and with different objectives, but with one common feature: the
willingness to use to violence.

The first category of terrorist groups
in Europe has been broadly decribed as
the 'New Left.' Students in the 1960s
were no longer content to question –
they challenged. The numbers of
students enjoying full-time further
education in the Western democracies
had mushroomed in the 1960s and the
educational institutions themselves
found it difficult to adapt. The children

of middle-class parents were developing
a sense of hostility to authority – in the
universities and more broadly, for some,
in society itself. They wanted change
and they were fully aware of the
philosophical contribution that Marxist
ideas could contribute to their ideals. It
was the era of demonstrations and of
protest marches on issues such as the
American involvement in the war in
Vietnam. The permissive society was
spawning a youthful generation with
ideals, ambitions and, it seemed for a
while, some real influence, especially
since political violence had become
intellectually respectable in some
circles. Mass action erupted in Paris in
the spring of 1968 and shook French
society, but only temporarily. Similar
demonstrations spread across Britain,

West Germany, Italy, America and
Japan. Yet the student activity, which in
some countries spread to other sections
of society, failed to bring about revolutionary change, leaving the more extreme minority frustrated and looking
for more radical methods to try to bring
about change. It was to terrorism that
they turned and to the works and
experience of guerrilla leaders like Che
Guevara and Régis Debray.

In the United States, the results of the
generation of confrontation were seen in
the Black Panther movement, the
Weathermen (an outgrowth from the
Students for a Democratic Society) and
ultimately the Symbionese Liberation
Army (SLA) in the 1970s. In Japan it
was the Japanese Red Army that became
responsible for the most horrifying
deeds, such as the massacre at Lod
Airport (Israel) in May 1972. In Britain
it was the Angry Brigade. The Brigade
emerged as a small group of amateur
revolutionaries who were hoping to
change the system overnight, carrying
out bomb attacks in the London area in
1970 and 1971. The Brigade belonged to
the anarchist fringe, and caused considerable damage to cars and property
but only one injury – to a woman on 31
July 1971 in an explosion outside the
residence of John Davies, Secretary of
State for Trade and Industry. By the end
of 1972 most of the activists were in

prison and the Brigade had ceased to operate. Similar student rebellion in France had been led by Daniel Cohn-Bendit. In May 1968 French riot police (the CRS) fought pitched battles with students in the streets of Paris which led to considerable sympathy for the demonstrators – but it was short-lived. The political effects were minimal and activity soon ceased. But in Italy and West Germany student rebellion lasted longer, despite the fact that there was little popular support and no really coherent ideology.

A radical student group centered upon the Free University of West Berlin, known as the Sozialistischen Deutscher Studentenbund (SDS), focused German attention on Berlin by organizing demonstrations against both the war in Vietnam and the Shah of Iran. Rudi Dutschke was a prominent and active member. But in 1967 a student was shot dead in riots in Berlin, and this prompted the creation of what was to become the Baader-Meinhof group. Its leading members, Gudrun Ensslin, Andreas Baader and Ulrike Meinhof, became totally committed to revolutionary philosophies and adopted the Latin American model of urban guerrilla warfare to try to destroy the structure of authority and wealth in capitalist West Germany. Their campaign was presaged in April 1968 by the planting of incendiary devices in two Frankfurt department stores; it was this that attracted Meinhof to join Ensslin and Baader. But Baader was arrested and imprisoned, leading to a dramatic rescue by Meinhof. This marked the real beginning of the Baader-Meinhof gang. After studying terrorism in the Middle East alongside the Palestinians in 1970 the group returned to Germany to organize its campaign, calling itself the Red Army Faction (RAF).

The year 1972 saw Baader-Meinhof bomb attacks on US military bases in Germany, on police officers and on the Axel Springer press building in Hamburg, by which time the gang had regional groups operating in different areas of West Germany. In response, the federal government created a special antiterrorist squad, the Grenzschütz Grüppen Nein (GSG9), increased the size of the police force, used infiltration

164

techniques while tightening security and passed new laws. This was condemned by the Left who claimed that they were afraid of the resulting concentration of power into the hands of the central government and the inevitable limitations placed on the individual freedom of the citizen. Many commentators on terrorism have deduced from this that some terrorist groups – like the RAF – deliberately set out with the objective of forcing a democratic and liberal government to introduce draconian measures which will undermine public support for it and gain sympathy for the revolutionary cause. In Germany, however, public sympathy was with the government. The results of the more sophisticated antiterrorist activity began to bear fruit when in 1972 Meinhof, Baader and Ensslin were all arrested. The trial of the three leaders and 18 other members was to take place at Stammheim outside Stuttgart, but it was not the end of the Baader-Meinhof gang.

Other terrorist groups had surfaced in West Germany, in particular one called the Second of June Movement – a radical group commemorating the death of the student in Berlin in 1967. Its members were involved in bombing and shooting incidents under the leadership of Ralf Reinders. In February 1975 they kidnapped Peter Lorentz, a West Berlin Christian Democrat, on the eve of the Berlin city elections. The government capitulated and released five RAF terrorists from prison – terms insisted

upon by the terrorists, clearly showing the pressure this sort of terrorism can pose for governments. Some of the people released were involved in terrorist activity later in 1975 and the lesson was not lost on the German or other governments. Terrorists cannot usually be bought off; to make concessions to terrorism merely encourages fanatics to resort to violence more willingly, since they then feel that they have a realistic chance of success. In April 1975 six terrorists took over the West German Embassy in Stockholm and held the Ambassador and his staff hostage. They demanded the release of Baader-Meinhof terrorists, but this time the government held firm, at the cost of two lives; nevertheless, something had been achieved. In December 1975 Baader-Meinhof supporters were involved in taking eleven oil ministers hostage at the OPEC meeting in Vienna, but again to no avail. In May 1976 the Baader-Meinhof gang suffered a serious blow when Ulrike Meinhof was found hanged in her cell in prison – the official verdict was suicide.

Another serious blow to the RAF occurred in June/July 1976 when, alongside terrorists of other nationalities, two Baader-Meinhof terrorists hijacked an Air France flight to Entebbe, only to be overwhelmed by an Israeli commando unit. The two were shot dead. But it was 1977 that proved to be a fateful year for the RAF. In April 1977 Siegfried Buback, the federal chief

Above: Dr Peter Lorentz, who was kidnapped in February 1975.
Above left: Jan-Carl Raspe (left) and Andreas Baader (right) at the start of the trial of the leading members of the Baader-Meinhof Gang in 1975.
Top far left: Johann Heinrich von Rauch was tried in Munich for terrorist acts including attempted murder.
Top center: Ulrike Meinhof of the Baader-Meinhof gang.
Top: Gudrun Ensslin, girlfriend of Baader, who killed herself in prison.
Left: German activist Rudi Dutschke.
Right: The West German Embassy in Stockholm, pictured after being rocked by two explosions, when Baader-Meinhof terrorists seized it and held nine people hostage, 1975.

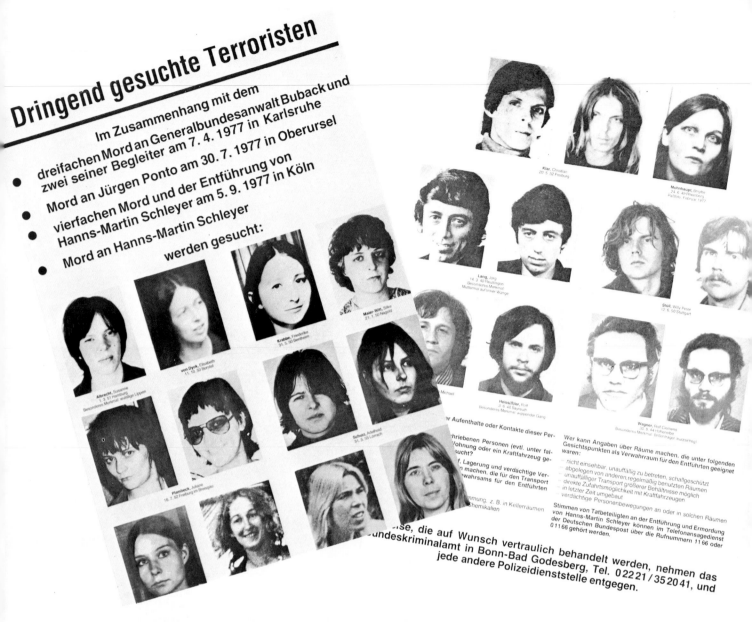

Dringend gesuchte Terroristen

Im Zusammenhang mit dem
- dreifachen Mord an Generalbundesanwalt Buback und zwei seiner Begleiter am 7. 4. 1977 in Karlsruhe
- Mord an Jürgen Ponto am 30. 7. 1977 in Oberursel
- vierfachen Mord und der Entführung von Hanns-Martin Schleyer am 5. 9. 1977 in Köln
- Mord an Hanns-Martin Schleyer

werden gesucht:

prosecutor in Karlsruhe, was ambushed and murdered just as the Stammheim trial of Baader, Ensslin and others was reaching its climax. The intention was to intimidate the authorities, but it did not prevent life sentences being imposed on the leaders in April. Kidnap and murder still continued – in July 1977 Dr Jurgen Ponti, a banker, was shot dead, and in September Hanns-Martin Schleyer, a business executive, was abducted. His fate was to be sealed by events thousands of miles from Germany, in Mogadishu, Somalia. On 13 October 1977 a Lufthansa Boeing 737 on a flight from Majorca to Frankfurt was hijacked and eventually flown to Mogadishu, where the terrorists asked for cash and the release of Baader-Meinhof prisoners. The West German government again stood firm, sending the GSG9 antiterrorist squad to storm the aircraft. The

terrorists were killed while all the passengers escaped – an important and symbolic victory for the authorities in trying to combat terrorism. Schleyer was subsequently found murdered, but as soon as the news of events at Mogadishu reached Stammheim, Baader was found shot and Ensslin hanged: again the verdicts were suicide. The Baader-Meinhof gang in effect died at Stammheim prison, for the security forces gradually succeeded in arresting the remaining members of the gang and have successfully prevented it from ever threatening West Germany again.

The West German experience with the Baader-Meinhof gang showed that citizens living in the vulnerable liberal democracies would put up with whatever measures were felt necessary to counter terrorism. Of particular significance was the increased effort made to

gather Intelligence through the use of modern technology like computer banks of information on suspects. The international links which the Red Army Faction had established also forced an international response, with greater co-operation between European authorities to try to combat terrorism by exchanging information gathered, and even with, as at Mogadishu where GSG9 was assisted by the British Special Air Service (SAS) Regiment, collaboration at the operational level. The techniques adopted by the RAF were symptomatic of the development of terrorist groups in the 1970s, as seen by the greater use of kidnapping and hostage-taking in comparison to the earlier widespread use of bombing and assassination. These techniques were guaranteed to provide publicity for the terrorist organization and its aims, as well as attempting to

166

Far left and left: A wanted poster for members of the urban guerrilla Red Army Faction, issued by the West German police in 1977.
Bottom: the 86 hijack victims arrive at Frankfurt after their dramatic rescue in Mogadishu, October 1977.
Right: The bullet-riddled bodies of Aldo Moro's driver and one of his bodyguards slumped on the front seats of Moro's car in Rome, March 1978, when urban terrorists of the Red Brigades abducted the Christian Democrat politician.
Below: Murdered by terrorists – Captain Juergen Schumann, pilot of the Lufthansa Boeing which was hijacked on a flight from Majorca to Frankfurt on 13 October 1977.

shift the responsibility for any subsequent deaths away from the terrorist group and onto the authorities and security forces concerned. A good example of this was the kidnapping of Aldo Moro in Italy in March 1978 by the Italian Red Brigades.

Italy has suffered from both Right- and Left-wing terrorism. Building upon a tradition of violence in Italy, and fanned by years of political scandal and corruption, Right-wing terrorist groups used bombs in Milan in 1969, killing 14, and in Bologna in 1980, killing 84. By far the most important terrorist group, however, was the *Brigate Rosse* – the Red Brigades – a Left-wing movement with obscure origins, but predominantly composed of disillusioned and frustrated Left-wing extremists. With a revolutionary zeal which they felt was missing from the Italian Communist Party, they resorted to an armed struggle against the ruling classes of Italian society, using kidnapping and assassination. Their operations began in 1974 after a period of preparation, during which they set up their organization and acquired training and arms through international terrorist

co-operation. They indulged in the kidnapping of magistrates and the assassination of important legal figures to try to force the release of prisoners. After the arrest for the second time of Renato Curcio – one of the Brigades' leaders – in January 1976, the Red Brigades resorted to the systematic murder of both magistrates and jurors in an attempt to prevent, by intimidation, the trial of Curcio.

The Italian Government and security forces were slow to rise to the challenge of terrorism, thereby encouraging its growth, so that by 1978 hardly a day went by in Italy without the occurrence of one or two new terrorist acts. But the events of 16 March 1978 finally pushed the Italian authorities into making an adequate response. The kidnapping in Rome of Aldo Moro, ex-prime minister and president of the Christian Democrat Party, was conducted in such a professional, cold-blooded and spectacular way, and ended in such brutal circumstances, that the Italian authorities finally took action. Desensitized by the frequency of political violence in the past decade, even the Italian people were

shocked at Moro's abduction and eventual fate.

The victim was being driven through Rome at a time when he was trying to forge a new coalition government in Italy with Communist Party participation. He had a driver and bodyguard in his car and a further two bodyguards in another car behind. But it was all to no avail – the Red Brigades had been planning the kidnap for months, and it worked. Moro was taken, leaving the cars and bodyguards behind in a scene of appalling brutality and blood. A coalition government was created that same day and they agreed not to enter into negotiations with Moro's captors, who wanted Curcio and others released. As time went by, Moro wrote increasingly bitter letters to his colleagues and friends – perhaps under duress – in criticism of the government's unyielding position. On 15 April, the Red Brigades' cell that had masterminded and organized the operation announced that Moro had been condemned to death by a 'people's trial,' and on 10 May his body was found in the boot of a car. The ordeal had lasted 54 days and turned to tragedy because

Above: The bearded leader of the Red Brigades, Renato Curcio, flanked by two of his followers, in a cage during their trial in Turin in 1978.
Left: Right-wing terrorists in Italy also caused indiscriminate damage and death: the remains of Bologna railroad station in August 1980. 84 people died after a bomb exploded.

neither the terrorists nor the government were prepared to give way. The terrorists had hoped that the government would be especially vulnerable to pressure because Moro was such an important figure, and that they would be forced to negotiate. However when they realized that this was not to be, their credibility was seriously challenged and the fanatical element won the argument over the fate of Moro. The episode caused horror and outrage throughout Italy, and prompted the creation of a special antiterrorist force drawn from the Carabinieri. Together with tougher legislation to outlaw terrorist groups, this provided Italian authorities with some success, since numerous arrests of both Right- and Left-wing groups followed. The number of terrorist acts dropped sharply after 1978, and the Red Brigades found that their actions had alienated the population rather than attracted more people into the movement and had brought revolution in Italy no nearer. Eventually the trials of the terrorists took place, surrounded by extremely tight security with the accused in cages inside court. This was,

however, to prove to be the last real publicity that the Red Brigade was able to attract.

Terrorism of this sort is extraordinarily resistant to serious theoretical analysis and there is no one theory of terrorism which manages to encompass the whole gamut of terrorist movements in Europe or elsewhere. Classification of terrorist groups is, however, possible and at the same time that Europe was encountering the upsurge of New Left terrorism, nationalist/separatist movements were also re-emerging and adopting similar types of tactics. This phenomenon was by no means unique to Europe, since in the Middle East the Palestinian nationalist movements were becoming very active, at the same time as separatists like the Front de Libération de Québec (FLQ) in Canada. In Europe, attention was focused on the revival of the IRA in Eire and Britain, and Euzkadi Ta Azkatasuna (ETA) in Spain. Most of these groups had little in common with the ideological roots of the New Left, and indeed little in common with each other save the underlying objective of national independence. In fact many such groups had religious overtones to their campaigns – the IRA and the PLO are good examples – and although there was some cross-fertilization between all these movements, the motivation of this group of terrorists was fundamentally nationalist in nature. The IRA aim was to unite all Ireland; the PLO wanted the creation of a Palestinian state and, for some, the concomitant destruction of the Zionist state of Israel. In Europe, both the IRA and ETA rejected the accusation that they were terrorist groups and, therefore, comparable with Baader-Meinhof or the Red Brigade. They claimed to be fighting a legitimate struggle for national independence. As 'freedom fighters,' therefore, their objectives were and still are limited and well understood, but it is nevertheless true that they have resorted to a campaign of terror to try to achieve their objectives.

The campaign launched by the IRA in 1970 was very much in the tradition of political violence experienced in Ireland in this century and before. In 1969 the Northern Ireland Civil Rights Association (NICRA) had organized protests

and demonstrations against the Protestant ascendancy in Ulster and some of its discriminatory effects against Catholics. Intercommunal violence escalated as the Protestants took to violence in response, and in August 1969 the British Army was moved in to act as a peacekeeping force in support of the Ulster security forces to try to uphold the rule of law and prevent the situation deteriorating into general sectarian violence right across the Province. At first the Army was greeted with relief by both sides of the community, but its presence on the streets of Northern Ireland soon prompted the old Irish nationalist ideas of an anti-British struggle, especially when it seemed that the role of the Army was to uphold the *status quo*, and in that sense, therefore, Protestant domination. Rioting and street violence escalated in 1970 so that the IRA was able to assume its traditional role in Ulster of attempting to protect Catholic areas from Protestant attack – since the demonstrations and riots had prompted Protestants to respond to what they perceived to be a threat to their dominant position.

The IRA itself, however, found it difficult to react as it was taken by surprise by the 1969 troubles. Its traditional commitment to the unification of Ireland through violence had led some parts of the IRA to adopt Marxist ideas and view Catholic and Protestant workers alike as being exploited by British control – a view that Ulster Protestants seemed to be distinctly unaware of, as were some members of the IRA. In 1970 the movement split into two, with the newly formed Provisional IRA breaking away from what became known as the Official IRA, leaving Marxist ideas to be subordinated to action in Northern Ireland. Both the Officials and the Provisionals have always maintained that their fight is with the British, not with the Protestants of Ulster, but the distinction is a fine one since Ulster Protestants are very firmly committed to unity with Britain – hence the use of the term 'Loyalists' to describe the Protestant majority in Northern Ireland. Nevertheless it was the Provisionals who went on to organize a systematic campaign of violence using terrorist tactics, with the result that Ulster suffered an escalation of indis-

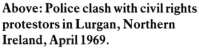

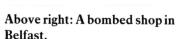

Above: Police clash with civil rights protestors in Lurgan, Northern Ireland, April 1969.
Right: British soldiers with CS gas pistols to quell rioters on the largely Protestant Shankill Road, Belfast, 1970.
Far right: Ulster policemen face youths in Londonderry in August 1969.

Above right: A bombed shop in Belfast.

criminate bombings of civilian targets and direct attacks on the police and the army. The Provisionals believed that the opportunity existed in the 1960s and 1970s to achieve their long-term objective of British withdrawal from Ulster.

As the Provisionals began to organize to defend Catholic areas in Ulster from Protestant attacks, they found the climate to be excellent for recruitment, with hundreds of volunteers emerging to bolster what was until then a tiny organization. Three brigades were set up in Belfast, Londonderry and the border counties in 1970, and as the army tried to counter rioting by the use of CS gas and house-to-house searches, young men and women joined the Provisionals. Arms and money were scarce, but it soon began to arrive from the United States via the Irish Northern Aid Association (NORAID). The Provisionals' targets were usually soldiers and police, as well as bombing of economic targets like business premises and shops. By 1971 the car bomb had become a popular device with the Provisionals even though it carried with it the danger of killing innocent passers-by. Indeed the bomb-

Above: Bloody Sunday; a youth is arrested by a paratrooper, the Bogside.
Above left: A paratrooper makes a rioter lie down to be searched.
Left: A foot patrol in Belfast.
Below: Protestant women outside Stormont demand firmer action against the IRA, May 1971.

ings, when they caused widespread civilian deaths, did shake Provisional support, but by and large the Provisionals could rely upon enough support among the Catholic population of Ulster to allow them to operate effectively.

The violence prevented efforts at a peaceful solution from having very much chance of success, and therefore to try to contain the escalating security problem, the authorities introduced internment in August 1971. This policy allowed for the arrest and indefinite custody without trial or charge of suspected terrorists; but Intelligence shortcomings meant that nonterrorists were picked up in the same net. It led to great resentment among the Catholic community, which in turn only served to push the violence to new levels, especially when stories of the mistreatment of detainees started to circulate. For the authorities, internment was to prove counterproductive, as events in 1972 were to illustrate. There were more riots, bombings and shootings; in the rural areas – especially in the border counties of Fermanagh, Tyrone and South Armagh – ambushes became more frequent and the security forces had to cope with the increased use of landmines, usually deployed in culverts running under roads. Policing in these predominantly Catholic border areas became impossible, with civil disobedience rife in terms of nonpayment of such things as license fees. Similarly in towns, neither the police nor the army could maintain a permanent presence in the 'No-Go' Catholic areas. Barricades were manned by the IRA, establishing IRA control over Catholic areas like the Bogside in Londonderry and the Falls Road in Belfast. The brutality of the IRA was not always approved of, but fear or dislike of the army and the Protestants made it acceptable, and this was a great boost to the effectiveness of the IRA.

The increased wave of urban terrorism was met by a firmer military stand, which culminated in tragedy on Sunday, 30 January 1972, when a riot developed during a march in Londonderry. Shots were fired and 13 civilians were killed. The army claimed that they were fired upon first; the IRA called it cold-blooded murder. Known as 'Bloody Sunday,' this episode outraged all Irish nationalist sentiment, IRA recruitment increased and the inevitable revenge occurred on 22 February when the Official IRA exploded a car bomb at the Aldershot barracks of The Parachute Regiment – the unit chiefly involved on 'Bloody Sunday.' It was the first IRA bomb explosion in England for over 30 years and marked the beginning of a new campaign. In Northern Ireland, however, the IRA achieved one of its long-standing objectives when the British government prorogued Stormont (the Ulster Parliament) in March 1972 and took over the government of Northern Ireland by direct rule, appointing a Secretary of State for the Province.

It was hoped that a new initiative for peace might succeed in the changed circumstances, especially when a truce was agreed and the IRA leadership was invited to talks with the London government, the first such talks for 50 years. The talks failed and have been controversial ever since. Did the British government give prestige and encouragement to the IRA cause by negotiating with them? It was certainly unusual for a government to sit down and talk with an organization which they regarded as a terrorist one. There followed more bombs and bloodshed. On 21 July 1972, known as 'Bloody Friday,' nine people were killed and 130 injured in a series of bombs in and around Belfast. Ten days later the army retaliated with Operation 'Motorman' and removed the 'No-Go' areas of Belfast and Londonderry.

As the army became more experienced, and as they collected more Intelligence, they and the police had greater success in capturing IRA gunmen and bombers, so much so that the IRA had to be reorganized in 1976-77. The old military structure of battalions and companies was abandoned as the Provisionals adopted the classic urban guerrilla structure of small cells. Each consisted of five to eight men and, as active service units (ASUs), they were far more secure than the older system, but their greater secrecy inevitably risked cutting them off from their local support in the Catholic community. But this did not prevent the IRA from initiating a bombing campaign in England.

Above left: Masked UDA men stand at one of the barricades that were set up in East Belfast to mark Protestant 'No-Go' areas, May 1972.
Below left: Soldiers on patrol, Belfast.

Above: IRA leaders in Londonderry, October 1972. Left to right, Martin McGuinness, David O'Connell, Sean McStiofain and Seamus Twomey.
Below: A lorry on fire during riots in the Falls Road, Belfast.

Above: Roy Jenkins (left), British Home Secretary, leaves the wrecked 'Horse and Groom' public house in Guildford, Surrey, after visiting the scene of IRA explosions in October 1974.

Public houses in Guildford and Birmingham were bombed in October and November 1974 respectively, causing many indiscriminate deaths. Attacks of this sort outside Ulster continued sporadically. In April 1974 Bridget Rose Dugdale and four armed men stole 19 paintings valued at $19.2 million from a British millionaire (who happened to be Dugdale's father) and theatened to destroy them. They demanded a ransom and the transfer to Northern Ireland prisons of IRA prisoners convicted of crimes in England, including the Price sisters jailed for the Old Bailey bombings in London. The paintings were recovered and Dugdale arrested and imprisoned. Later in October 1975 Eddie Gallagher (Dugdale's common-law husband) and Marion Coyle kidnapped Dutch businessman Teide Herrema in Dublin and demanded the release of Dugdale. Eventually Gallagher and Coyle surrendered and Herrema was rescued, with Gallagher later being imprisoned himself.

In Northern Ireland, the widespread and serious violence of 1972 has never since been matched. Bombing and murders continued – for example, of the judiciary in their homes in Belfast in 1974 – but in 1975 terrorist activity declined except for some sectarian tit-for-tat killings. This led to a bloody feud inside the Republican movement, and another group, calling itself the Irish Republican Socialist Party, broke away from the Official IRA to form its own military wing, the Irish National Liberation Army (INLA), demanding more action in Northern Ireland to drive out the British. The importance of the emergence of the INLA was its fanaticism. It was small and influenced by Marxism, with a young ambitious element keen to progress more quickly with the political campaign of violence, which made it more akin to many Western European terrorist organizations. It had good contacts with the PLO and Libya and managed to acquire arms and explosives which it employed selectively to devastating effect. Admittedly, the split resulted in battles and killings between INLA and the Official IRA and between the Officials and the Provisionals, but most violence was still intercommunal.

The Protestants of Northern Ireland, in order to defeat the IRA, remain in the United Kingdom and to prosecute reprisals, have seen fit to create their own paramilitary movements, some of which have, like the IRA, resorted to the use of

lieve that it can use terrorism to intimidate the Protestants. The Red Hand Commandos and the UFF were both made illegal after admitting to the bombing and shooting of Catholics. By the 1980s the Protestant Action Force was most active in the campaign against Catholics. The Protestant paramilitaries, although existing and occasionally operating with terror tactics, will only have a major impact if the issue of a united Ireland becomes a real possibility, but they are a threatening contribution to the peculiarly complex pattern of Northern Irish politics and security.

Attempts at political progress during this time, as before, all failed, chiefly because of the unwillingness of either side to compromise. Power-sharing at one time seemed to be a possible solution but it was wrecked by the Ulster Workers Council strike of May 1974 – which graphically displayed Protestant displeasure at the idea of power-sharing with the Catholics and also showed the Protestants' power to prevent progress if they felt so inclined. Other similar attempts were no more successful.

British policy in Northern Ireland changed in the mid-1970s, having weathered and learned from the experience of 1969-72. Internment ceased in 1975, much to the relief of almost everyone concerned, and in 1976 special-category status was also ended. This meant that terrorists would be treated as criminals in the normal way and given no privileges because of the political motivation of their crimes. This move, although bitterly resented by the IRA, removed another source of legitimacy and romanticism that nationalist movements try to cultivate. The government in London has also pursued an 'Ulsterization' policy, which entails handing back to Ulster as much as possible of the daily administration of local affairs and to use the Ulster Defence Regiment (UDR) and RUC wherever and whenever possible for patrolling and general duties. In this way the British Army presence has been reduced gradually but significantly from the peak in 1972 of 21,000 to 12,000 in the early 1980s, so as to make the overall effect of direct rule from London as palatable as possible to the Ulster population. The ending of special-category status triggered a

Above: Men of the Loyalist UVF at a press conference in Belfast.
Top left: The paramilitary UDA on patrol in Protestant areas of Belfast.
Above left: The bomb attack at Warrenpoint, County Down, 1970.

terrorism. There were always some Protestants who were willing to organize direct action against the Catholics if they thought the government was taking a conciliatory line with the nationalists. In 1966 Protestant fanatics formed the Ulster Volunteer Force (UVF), which was responsible for sectarian murders and was, therefore, banned by the government. In 1971 the Ulster Defence Association (UDA) was formed and was seen on the streets of Northern Ireland from 1972 onward. This led to an increased sectarian murder campaign which the security forces had to combat, necessitating the internment of Protestants as well. The Protestant paramilitaries and smaller organizations like the Red Hand Commandos and the Ulster Freedom Fighters (UFF) want to make it clear that the people of Ulster will not contemplate a united Ireland and that the IRA is, therefore, mistaken to be-

Above: The response to urban rioting: British troops, sheltered by an adapted Humber 'Pig,' rush forward to break up a crowd, Londonderry, 1980.
Below: A specially trained sniffer dog is used to check for car bombs.

Right: A British soldier stands in front of a typical piece of Belfast 'wall art.' Such graffiti is a useful method of spreading the Republican message.

Below: A member of the Royal Ulster Constabulary uses a street corner for cover in case of IRA snipers. The use of a civilian police force, albeit armed, is often essential if an air of near normality is to be sustained.

nationalist response inside the prisons of Northern Ireland with, firstly, the blanket protests, followed by the dirty protests and a wave of hunger strikes in 1980 and 1981 which resulted in the death of Bobby Sands on 5 May 1981 and gained worldwide publicity.

The IRA and INLA returned to a campaign of bombing and assassination in England in the late 1970s, in the hope that the British commitment to Northern Ireland was less than firm and that one bomb in England would be worth ten in Northern Ireland. Incendiary devices and bombs appeared in London in 1977 and 1979. The INLA made their first serious appearance with the assassination of the Conservative spokesman on Northern Ireland, Airey Neave, on 30 March 1979. In the Irish Republic, Lord Mountbatten was assassinated by a bomb in his boat at Mullaghmore on 27 August 1979, and on the same day 18 British soldiers were killed by a huge explosion at Warrenpoint, north of the border. There were occasional bomb attacks in 1980 and 1981, but most attention was focused on the hunger strikes, which won the IRA some public sympathy among the Catholic population of Northern Ireland and abroad, where sympathy meant increased financial aid. In October 1981, however, a nail bomb was exploded outside Chelsea barracks, closely followed by other bombs in London and especially in the shopping area of Oxford Street. In July 1982 bombs were placed at the Regents Park bandstand and in Hyde Park, causing nine deaths, and in December 1983 a car bomb at Harrod's department store in London killed five. In October 1984 Irish nationalists were almost successful in assassinating Prime Minister Margaret Thatcher with a bomb in the Grand Hotel, Brighton, where most of the government were staying during the Conservative Party Conference. Irish terrorists are now masters of bombing techniques, with the increasing use of remote-controlled mechanisms. The Brighton bomb seems to show how easily-available delayed-timing mechanisms (as found in modern video recorders, for example) can be adapted to provide preset and, with other precautions, undetectable devices.

The ability of Irish nationalist terror-

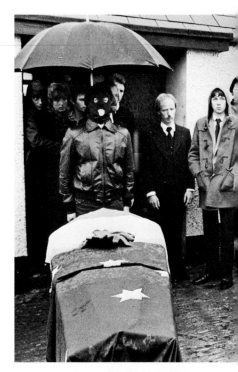

ists, therefore, to inflict damage in Northern Ireland and England is unquestioned and probably impossible to prevent, although antiterrorist precautions and techniques are increasingly able to contain such a campaign. It is equally true that the bombing campaign in England has not had the required effect, since the British government is as firm as ever in refusing to contemplate any changes to the status of Northern Ireland without the agreement of the majority of the inhabitants of the Province. Also Irish nationalist groups cannot be wholly prevented from continuing to operate backwards and forwards across the border from Eire to Northern Ireland, using rural guerrilla warfare tactics, but again, the security forces can contain such a threat. In Northern Ireland itself, urban guerrilla warfare and terrorist attacks by the IRA and INLA cannot be completely prevented without resorting to draconian measures, but there may be a limit to the willingness of the local population to continue to allow violence to be perpetrated in their midst. The Provisional IRA, which again became linked to Marxism in the early 1980s, has shown itself to be adaptable; it has solid roots in the Irish nationalist movement and is unlikely to give up its campaign. It has found terrorism to be a useful weapon.

In somewhat similar circumstances,

Above: Masked INLA men flank a
woman as she fires over the coffin of
James Mallon, County Armagh.
Above left: The death of an IRA
hunger striker is signalled in the Falls
Road, Belfast.
Left: The Grand Hotel, Brighton, after
the IRA bomb attack in October 1984.

the Basque nationalist movement ETA
has also resorted to the use of terrorism
in Spain. The modern Basque nationalist movement was formed in the late
nineteenth century to further the cause
of autonomy for the 1,000,000 people
living in the seven provinces of northern
Spain and part of southwest France that
is traditionally the home of the Basques.
Prosperous today, the Basques suffered
repression during the Franco years, and
in 1959 extremists broke away from the
nationalist movement to form ETA. It is
a linguistic and cultural movement, with
a political wing – similar to Sinn Fein in
Ireland – called *Herri Batasuna*. The
military wing, *ETA militar*, became rest-
less and resorted to a campaign of terrorism in 1967 with the police, army,
government officials and public installations the usual targets for violence.
Franco reacted by attempting to repress
the Basques even more, which only led
to increased support for ETA. Like the
IRA, ETA also espoused Marxist ideology, and talked of a socialist republic,

and there is a sense in which revolution
in Spain had become an important priority. ETA, therefore, forged links with
other terrorist organizations like the
PLO and the IRA; indeed, the explosive
that was used to assassinate the Spanish
Premier, Admiral Luis Carrero Blanco,
in Madrid on 20 December 1973 came
from the Provisional IRA. This murder
was one of ETA's most daring and had
taken months to plan by the digging of a
tunnel under the road in which the explosive was placed. Blanco's car was
lifted five stories upward by the blast.

In November 1975 General Franco
died and Spain passed relatively easily
into a civilian democracy headed by
King Juan Carlos. The government began to lift the repression of the Basques;
in 1979 devolution provided for a
regional government at Vittoria and a
remarkable degree of autonomy inside
the Spanish monarchy. Moderate
Basque nationalist opinion, including
the Basque Nationalist Party, has
generally found this to be acceptable,
but the full text of the law to provide
autonomy has not yet been implemented. ETA, in its revolutionary
phase, attempted to escalate the armed
struggle so as to try to prevent the
government from introducing this compromise – they even turned on moderate
Basque nationalists, who were condemned as traitors. The number of
deaths that ETA has claimed responsibility for (and they are mostly army,
police and businessmen) increased considerably from 19 in 1976 to 130 in 1979.

The dedicated hard-core militants of
ETA number around 200 or so, and in
recent times they have been increasingly
isolated in the Basque community, even
to the extent of demonstrations taking
place against terrorism. Nevertheless,
the cell structure of ETA gives it the
ability to survive despite this declining
local sympathy. Equally important to
ETA is the long frontier with the neighboring democracy of France – again very
similar to the situation found in Ireland –
with the useful sanctuary that southwest
France provides. An extradition agreement between France and Spain will be
necessary to solve this problem and it is a
real problem, especially since 1980,
when the Spanish antiterrorist force
caused a diplomatic incident by shooting

two terrorists in a bar in France.

Spain's antiterrorist effort has now
improved, but the Guardia Civil is hated
in the Basque area and its presence deeply resented. The Spanish government's
efforts are aided by an organization
called GAL – an antiterrorist liberation
group – which has been involved in
assassinating terrorists. The government's policy is based on using maximum firmness against terrorists while
giving every incentive, adding up almost
to amnesty, to all those terrorists who
come forward and renounce violence.
There are signs of some success – unlike
in Ireland where the political situation is
stagnant. However, like the IRA, it is
difficult to see the fanatical nationalist
element of ETA giving up, whatever the
Spanish government offers.

Europe has not only suffered from
European-based terrorism, whether
New Left or nationalist, however, for it
has also been used as a playground for
international terrorism and as a suitable
target for non-European terrorist movements. In fact a very large proportion of
terrorist acts committed in Europe have
their roots in the Middle East, and in
particular with the Palestinians, although the Libyans and Iranians have
also been active. The campaign made
use of the assistance given by New Left
movements in Europe and vice versa;
Europeans were trained to handle
weapons and explosives in the Middle
East and Palestinians and Europeans co-
operated on operations. Indeed, Europe
was the scene of one of the most horrific
terrorist attacks seen to this day, when
Palestinian terrorists were responsible
for the deaths of 11 members of the
Israeli team at the Munich Olympics in
September 1972. Munich encouraged
European states to make a concerted
effort to try to combat terrorism. What
emerged was the EEC Six-Point
Counter-Terrorism Agreement of 1976,
supplemented by the Council of
Europe's Convention on Terrorism in
1977. International agreements have
been sparse in this field, since governments take up such diverging opinions
about what can or should be done to
counter terrorist activity.

Many early episodes of terrorism in
Europe were masterminded by the leading Arab activist in Europe, the Algerian

Mohammed Boudia, who, as early as March 1971, had been involved in blowing up oil installations of Gulf Oil in Rotterdam. In June 1973 he was assassinated, probably by the Israelis, in a car-bomb explosion in Paris, and this enabled Ilich Ramirez Sanchez, a Venezuelan known as 'Carlos,' to take over as the leader of international terrorism in Europe, and to assist the PFLP in its operations in Europe in particular. It was 'Carlos' who led the terrorists who took hostage the OPEC ministers at the meeting in Vienna in December 1975 – a daring and flamboyant act. But the international character of terrorism was not simply the result of ideological conviction; it was also practical. It provided the opportunity for different terrorist movements to exchange information, co-ordinate operations, train personnel in the use of arms and explosives, and to move arms and personnel across borders.

Some European countries have found themselves uncomfortably hosting acts of international terrorism. In September 1974, for example, terrorists belonging to the Japanese Red Army seized eleven hostages in the French Embassy in The Hague, asking for money and the release of terrorists held in prison in France. The terrorists' demands were met in this instance, but the Dutch government no doubt resented the fact that terrorism of this sort should involve them in such difficult circumstances; no state can be sure that its territory will not be used for terrorist acts. The Dutch must have been less surprised to find that on 2 December 1975 a South Moluccan terrorist group hijacked a train in Holland, killing the driver and taking the passengers hostage. The islands of South Molucca had been part of the Dutch East Indies and there was a sizeable South Moluccan population living in the Netherlands, some of whom supported the idea of national independence. Two days later, on 4 December, another group of South Moluccans occupied the Indonesian consulate in Amsterdam, taking Dutch and Indonesian hostages. The train hijackers shot one of their hostages and dumped the body out of the door of the train on to the railroad tracks, but eventually negotiations persuaded them to surrender and all the

Above: Gen Quintana, killed by ETA terrorists, 29 January 1984.
Left: A Basque gunman, reputedly one of those responsible for the assassination of Carrero Blanco.

other hostages on the train and in the Embassy were released. The problem occurred again in May 1977 when another train was hijacked and the pupils of a primary school held hostage. The Dutch government ruled out negotiations about the release of jailed South Moluccans in Holland; eventually the schoolchildren were released and the train was stormed by Dutch Marines, resulting in the death of six terrorists and two hostages. A third episode in March 1978, when government offices were taken over in Assen by South Moluccans, was similarly ended by Marine assault, since when the Dutch government has taken constructive steps to minimize South Moluccan frustration over their cause by improving housing conditions and schooling.

Europe provides, therefore, a classic study of the multifarious nature of terrorism and international terrorism. There have been occasions in Europe when terrorism has been used to gain publicity, to achieve the release of fellow terrorists, to obtain finance, to provoke the authorities into over-reaction or to blackmail governments. Some groups have been inspired by ideology, others by nationalism and some by revenge. Some groups have used assassination, others expropriation, kidnapping, hijacking and bombing. Yet if the zenith of terrorism in Europe seems to have occurred in the 1970s, that is only to say that the incidence of terrorist attacks has declined somewhat since then. Some of the Far Left movements are probably dead and gone, but others may be dormant, and there is endless potential for nationalist movements in Europe to adopt terrorist tactics should they so decide. Emulation of other groups has been a potent driving force, especially during the 1970s, but terrorist groups probably need to 'succeed' to encourage or spawn others, and the record is not promising. As counterterrorist techniques have been perfected by most European governments, 'success' becomes more difficult to achieve. The firm stand taken against terrorism by most European governments has shown rewards, but in the long run terrorism in Europe as elsewhere can only be contained, not entirely eliminated.

7. TOWARDS THE FUTURE

The role of the guerrilla in the modern world is notoriously difficult to assess. 'One man's guerrilla is another man's freedom fighter' may be a cliché, but it still rings true: to some people the guerrilla is a murderer, a bandit or a terrorist, while to others he is a liberator, a savior or a symbol of national independence. What cannot be denied, however, is that guerrilla warfare has had, and continues to have, a substantial impact on the politics of individual states. Many countries, including China, Vietnam, Cuba and Nicaragua,

owe their present political and social frameworks to the guerrilla; others, such as Uruguay, El Salvador and Afghanistan, have been significantly affected by their efforts to contain or counter his techniques.

This impact is all the more noticeable because of the development of guerrilla aims and methods over the last 50 years. Before World War II, guerrilla warfare was usually described as little more than a response to conventional military defeat or enemy occupation; a 'last-ditch' effort to salvage national pride or harass an alien force. Thus the Boer commandos, although effective guerrillas, only resorted to such tactics after having been defeated by the British in

open battle in 1899-1900 and they recognized from the start of their campaign that they would never be able to achieve complete victory against the full might of a mobilized imperial power. The best they could hope to do was to make continued British deployment so costly that a less-than-crushing political settlement could be negotiated. Similarly, despite occasional successes, the resistance or partisan groups which sprang up in response to German, Italian or Japanese occupation during World War II rarely imagined that they would be able to liberate their own states, realizing that such a result could only be achieved through the full-scale commitment of a replacement or allied field army and the

The continuing face of guerrilla war: Afghan fighters pose atop a derelict Soviet-manufactured BTR-60PB APC.

conventional defeat of the enemy occupying force, suitably weakened and stretched by guerrilla assaults. The techniques adopted by these guerrillas – hit-and-run attacks, ambushes, assassinations and sabotage – may be familiar to their modern-day successors, but at the time they represented nothing more than the natural reaction of patriots faced with the apparently invulnerable nature of a conventional army. Using and exploiting their advantages of tactical surprise, local knowledge and popular support, such 'traditional' guerrillas may be described as proponents of the lowest common denominator of warfare.

Mao Tse-tung was the first to recognize that this could be taken one stage further, and he did so by incorporating the 'natural' elements of guerrilla warfare into the wider politico-military needs of a revolution. His gradual evolution of ideas and, perhaps more importantly, his success in China by 1949, acted as a model, blueprint and inspiration to other revolutionary groups, some of which – the Viet Minh/Viet Cong in Vietnam, the *fidelistas* in Cuba and the host of nationalist movements which emerged throughout the disintegrating empires of the Western powers in the 1950s and 1960s – succeeded in using similar techniques to ensure a favorable outcome to their campaigns. It is worth stressing, however, that Mao said virtually nothing that was new about guerrilla warfare as such; he did not alter the tactics or the preconditions of the 'traditional' pattern, but merely used it as an integral part of his revolutionary process. His three-phase campaign in China, beginning with the nonmilitary aim of gaining popular support in a remote 'safe base' area and ending with the equally nonmilitary process of a usurpation of political power, used guerrilla techniques to wear down the morale and effectiveness of superior government forces, creating a situation in which the strengths of those forces – their firepower, cohesion and discipline – were gradually undermined as they were forced to dissipate resources in response to a demoralizing 'war in the shadows.' Even then, Mao made it clear that the guerrillas could only affect a stage in the

Above: Not all Afghans are guerrillas: a pro-Soviet parade in Kabul, 1980. Right: An Afghan soldier, armed with a folding-stock Kalashnikov assault rifle, poses amid the wreckage of a government convoy, hit by the guerrillas, 1980.

Above right: The Afghan Army in training, 1981. Despite Soviet support and arms, the government forces have found it hard to compile a successful response to the politico-religious appeal of the Mujahaddin.

developing revolution; final victory would come after the guerrillas had been organized into conventional formations, capable of confronting and defeating the government army in open battle. In that sense, little had changed.

Nevertheless, some spectacular successes may be attributed to the Maoist theory. China is the most obvious, producing a revolution which, despite Mao's talk of a 'protracted war' lasting generations, took only 22 years to reach fruition. Within five more years, Vietnamese communists under Ho Chi Minh and Vo Nguyen Giap had followed a similar pattern to rid the northern provinces of their state from the imperialist rule of the French, and this proved to be merely a precursor to continued revolutionary activity that was to culminate in 1975 with complete communist victory in South Vietnam, Laos and Cambodia (Kampuchea). Elsewhere, other attempts may not have enjoyed such success, in Malaya (1948-60) and the Philippines (1946-54), for example, Maoist-style revolutionaries failed to achieve their aims. However, the examples of China and North Vietnam seemed to suggest that by the mid-1950s a new, virtually indestructible process of social and political change, spearheaded by guerrilla action, had emerged.

But the successes as well as the failures implied that the Maoist pattern was not necessarily applicable to all areas of the globe. Indeed, the consensus was that Mao's ideas could only be extended effectively to countries which bore a resemblance to (and preferably shared a common border with) the China of the 1930s and 1940s. Unfortunately such conditions could not be guaranteed. Only a select number of states, for example, contained areas remote enough to house 'safe bases' free from the prying eyes of government forces, while others lacked the socio-political grievances so essential to the revolutionary process or were protected by security forces capable of responding to the developing threat. Mao had been extremely fortunate in the fact that Chiang Kai-shek could afford neither the resources nor the manpower to concentrate against the communist menace once the Japanese had attacked his state, and the Viet Minh

Below: A pro-government Iban tribesman guards suspected guerrilla infiltrators, Borneo, 1965.
Above right: A machine gun manned by Gurkhas of the British Army in Borneo, 1965.

Above: Members of Hissène Habré's Forces Armées du Nord, with AK-47s, central Chad, 1981. Civil war has been endemic in Chad since 1960; these guerrillas now support the government, Habré having seized power in June 1982.

were lucky in that they were facing an enemy already demoralized, both politically and militarily, by its defeats in Europe during World War II, but elsewhere the pattern was broken. In Malaya, for example, the British colonial authorities proved capable not only of recognizing the techniques of Maoist revolution but also of countering them in the remote jungle areas where the revolutionaries should have been safe. It was the sort of sobering defeat that opened up a crack in the seemingly invulnerable façade of Maoist-style revolt.

As such failures began to emerge, revolutionaries looked for an alternative approach, designed in most cases to ensure the development of guerrilla operations regardless of the level of political preparation. This seemed to work in Cuba between 1956 and 1959, when Fidel Castro virtually dispensed with the 'safe base' concept once his guerrillas had survived government attacks in the Sierra Maestra mountains of Oriente province, but it proved to be a false trail, inapplicable to other campaigns. Castro, like Mao and Ho Chi Minh before him, enjoyed a large measure of unique good fortune, in this

case arising from the fact that his political opponent in Cuba, Fulgencio Batista, was already isolated and intensely unpopular. This left the center of political power extremely vulnerable to even the smallest amount of guerrilla pressure, implying that, in similar circumstances elsewhere in Latin America, all that was needed for success was strong guerrilla leadership and dedicated revolutionary rank and file. Indeed, Che Guevara took this process to its extreme, arguing that the revolutionary cadre, acting as a focus for all the discontents of society, could actually create a revolutionary situation even where one did not exist before, and it was to take a plethora of failures throughout Latin America in the mid-1960s, culminating in Che's abortive (and fatal) expedition to Bolivia in 1967, for the theory to be completely discredited.

But the revolutionaries did not give up, desperately searching for a new formula as the frustration of constant failure increased. In Latin America, where the population was shifting dramatically away from the rural areas into the cities, this produced a trend

toward urban guerrilla warfare, initially in an attempt to take the pressure off the rural revolutionaries but soon to find among the dispossessed slum-dwellers the raw material of a potentially successful campaign. In itself, this was nothing new – after all, the Russian Revolution of 1917 had drawn the bulk of its support from the oppressed industrial proletariat, unavoidably concentrated in the cities, and nationalist campaigns in both Ireland (1916-21) and Cyprus (1955-59) had used urban tactics – but the aim remained that of Mao: the usurpation of political power through the gradual wearing down of security forces and government support. Once again, the process was difficult to put into effect, particularly as by now it bore little resemblance to the original Maoist pattern. Targets in the cities may have been easier to find and, initially, to hit, but they elicited the sort of immediate government response that Mao had avoided during the first two phases of revolutionary war and, as Castro had predicted in the early 1960s, the city in many cases became 'the graveyard of the revolutionaries and resources.' It was another blind alley.

The deep sense of frustration which resulted must be seen as one of the root causes of the spread of terrorism as an alternative technique. Once again, it was by no means a novel development; terrorism as such had been a tactic of political persuasion for centuries and had found a place in most guerrilla campaigns, including those of Mao in China and Ho Chi Minh in Vietnam, but the fact that it became such a central feature of revolution in the late 1960s/ early 1970s implies a failure of other methods. Nor should this be particularly surprising. Terrorism – the attempt to affect people's attitudes, actions and allegiances through the imposition of deep fear in their minds – is a relatively easy option, for once a terrorist has made the necessary moral adjustment, he enjoys a sense of freedom, particularly in the liberal democracies of the West, that allows him to perpetrate acts that would normally be constrained by the limits of civilized behavior. The planting of bombs in public places, the hijacking of aircraft or trains, the kidnap and murder of selected victims are all techniques which require little preparation and do not depend for success upon the sort of sophisticated political infrastructure advocated by Mao. In a very real sense, terrorism is 'theater,' designed to present society with such shocking and seemingly irrational acts that it will be forced to take notice, blaming the government for allowing them to occur and gradually preparing the way for a 'climate of collapse' out of which the new society of the revolutionaries will eventually emerge. The pattern was made infinitely more complex and threatening by the adoption of similar techniques by the various nationalist groups (countered in their guerrilla campaigns by effective government response) as well as the New Left in the late 1960s. Links between all three strands of terrorism – the revolutionaries of Latin America, epitomized in the activities of the Venezuelan 'Carlos,' the nationalists such as the PLO, PFLP and IRA, and the New Left represented by groups such as the Baader-Meinhof Red Army Faction and the Japanese Red Army – served to increase their impact, although not necessarily their effectiveness. The liberal democracies, whose very freedoms left them uniquely vulnerable to such attacks, succeeded in containing the worst of the violence, chiefly by refusing to be intimidated and by mounting selected counterstrikes of their own. By the early 1980s, in the aftermath of Entebbe, Mogadishu and the Iranian Embassy siege in London, the level of international terrorism had declined. Individual acts continued to be carried out – some, such as the hijacking of the Kuwaiti airliner to Tehran in December 1984, with increased levels of personal violence – but the threat had been diminished.

It would therefore seem logical to conclude that, although the use of guerrilla techniques has changed since 1945 and a number of states have been forced into political change as a result of revolutionary guerrilla campaigns, the basic role of the guerrilla has suffered little alteration. Indeed, it would be possible to argue that guerrilla warfare has been largely discredited in the inexorable round of failure, first in the rural areas, then in the cities and most recently in the international sphere of terrorism. But that should not be taken to mean that guerrillas are no longer a viable force. The guerrilla is still around: the reasons for his emergence may change, the demands of insurgents may be more strident or, reflecting frustration, more nihilistic, and the methods employed may be more immediately effective as a result of new technology, but the basic principles of guerrilla warfare remain attractive, especially to a minority within a state who decide to confront the conventional strengths of established military forces. For this reason it may be no coincidence that the guerrilla groups that have survived – the IRA in Northern Ireland, the Basques in Spain, the Palestinians in the Middle East – are the ones in which the desire for national self-determination is strong. They were always the types of group to which guerrilla techniques were second nature. A few might have toyed with the idea of international links and all have adopted the tactics of terrorism to gain instantaneous public recognition, but in the end they are fighting the sort of campaign which the Boers or the Russian partisans would have recognized: a low-level military response to alien rule, designed to wear down resolve rather than defeat the enemy in open battle. In the process they have adopted the best of the techniques experimented with elsewhere – a mix of rural, urban and international operations – and this may well be the pattern of the future.

RECOMMENDED READING

Asprey, R *War in the Shadows* (New York, 1975)

Becker, J *Hitler's Children, The Story of the Baader-Meinhof Gang* (London, 1977)

Beckett, I and Pimlott, J (ed) *Armed Forces and Modern Counter-Insurgency* (London, 1985)

Bruce, N *Portugal: The Last Empire* (Newton Abbot, 1975)

Cobban, H *The Palestinian Liberation Organisation* (Cambridge, 1984)

Coogan, T P *The I.R.A.* (London, 1980)

Debray, R *Che's Guerrilla War* (London, 1975)

Dobson, C and Payne, R *The Carlos Complex* (London, 1977)

Dunkerley, J *The Long War: Dictatorship & Revolution in El Salvador* (London, 1982)

Fairbain, G *Revolutionary Guerrilla Warfare. The Countryside Version* (London, 1974)

Foot, M R D *Resistance* (London, 1976)

Gott, R *Rural Guerrillas in Latin America* (London, 1973)

Grivas, G *Guerrilla Warfare* (London, 1964)

Guevara, E (Che). *Reminiscences of the Cuban Revolutionary War* (London, 1968)

Guevara, E (Che). *Guerrilla Warfare* (London, 1972)

Horne, A *A Savage War of Peace. Algeria, 1954-1962 (London, 1977)*

Laqueur, W *Guerrilla. A historical and critical study* (London, 1977)

Laqueur, W *Terrorism* (London, 1977)

Lawrence, T E *Seven Pillars of Wisdom* (London, 1935)

Mao Tse-tung *Selected Military Writings* (Peking, 1967)

Marighela, C *For the Liberation of Brazil* (London, 1971)

Mickolus, E F *Transnational Terrorism. A Chronology of Events, 1968-1979* (London, 1980)

Moorcraft, P and McLaughlin, P *Chimurenga! The War in Rhodesia, 1965-1980* (Johannesburg, 1982)

Moss, R *Urban Terrorism* (London, 1973)

Orbis, *War in Peace Part-work* (London, 1983-85)

Paget, J *Counter-Insurgency Campaigning* (London, 1967)

Taber, R *The War of the Flea* (London, 1972)

Thompson, R (ed) *War in Peace* (London, 1981)

Index

Page numbers in italics refer to illustrations

Acknowledgments

The publisher would like to thank the individuals and agencies listed below, who supplied the photographs:
ADN: pages 49 (bottom), 51 (bottom), 53 (inset).
AFP: page 60 (top).
Associated Press: pages 57 (top), 61 (top), 114 (top), 115 (top), 117 (bottom), 118 (both), 120/1, 122 (all three), 124 (top right), 125, 126 (all three), 127, 128 (both), 130 (both), 131, 134, 135 (both), 136-7 (all three), 149 (middle), 150/1 (top), 160 (both), 162/3, 163 (both), 164 (bottom), 165 (middle), 167 (top), 168, 184/5, 188 (top).
BBC Hulton Picture Library: pages 8 (left), 21 (all three), 22 (top right & bottom left), 22 (bottom), 22/3 (both).
Belfast Telegraph: pages 172/3, 173, 174 (top).
Bison Picture Library: pages 51 (top), 52/3 (both), 156, 186-7 (all three).
CTK: page 45.
China Photo Service: page 46 (top).
Cuban Embassy, London: pages 106/7, 107 (inset), 110 (bottom).
ECPA: pages 66/7.
Haganah Archives: page 143 (top).
Helmoed-Römer Heitman: pages 95 (both), 98/9 (main photo & inset left and middle).
Impact Photos/Philippe Achache: pages 90 (top right), 111 (bottom).
Impact Photos/Alain le Garsmeur: pages 2/3, 102/3, 129 (both), 158/9, 174 (bottom), 175 (both), 178 (top & bottom left), 179.
Impact Photos/Homer Sykes: pages 132/3.
Imperial War Museum: pages 18 (top), 18/19, 19 (top), 20, 24 (both), 25 (all three), 27 (left top & bottom), 28/9, 64 (top), 68 (both), 69, 70 (bottom), 71 (bottom), 92 (bottom), 140 (bottom), 141 (both), 161

(bottom), 162 (left), 188 (bottom), 189.
Israel Defence Force Archive: page 138 (bottom).
Israeli Government Press Office: pages 146 (top left & top right), 147 (top), 153 (bottom right), 154-5 (all four), 156-7 (all four).
Jabotinsky Institute: pages 139 (bottom left & right), 143 (bottom).
Mansell Collection: pages 9, 13, 22 (top right).
Maritime Museum, Cape Town: pages 16 (bottom), 17 (bottom left).
Maxwell's Photo Agency, Dublin: page 170 (top right).
National Army Museum: pages 11, 12 (bottom), 14, 32.
Richard Natkiel: pages 12 (top), 22 (top left), 35 (bottom), 56, 63 (top), 70 (top), 106 (inset), 140 (top).
Peter Newark's Western Americana: pages 8 (right), 16 (top), 17 (bottom right), 32, 33 (top right), 35 (top middle & top right), 39 (top), 40 (top), 166 (both).
Pacemaker Press Agency: pages 170 (top left & bottom), 172 (top), 175 (top left), 176 (both), 178 (bottom right), 180 (top), 180/81.
Paratus: page 94 (top).
The Photo Source/Central Press: pages 48 (both), 71 (top), 73, 88/9, 91 (bottom), 92 (top), 124 (top left), 172 (bottom), 175 (top right), 182.
The Photo Source/Fox: page 35 (top left).
The Photo Source/Keystone: pages 4/5, 33 (top left & bottom), 34, 36/7, 38, 39 (bottom), 40/41, 42 (top inset), 44 (both), 46 (bottom), 46/7, 49 (top), 63 (bottom), 64 (bottom left & bottom right), 65 (both), 68 (bottom), 69 (bottom), 72, 74 (both), 76-7 (all four), 78, 78/9 (both), 80, 81 (both), 82, 83, 84-5 (all four), 86-7 (all four), 89 (inset), 90 (top left, top middle & bottom), 91 (top), 93, 96, 97, 101, 104-5 (all four), 109 (top), 114 (bottom), 115 (bottom), 116/7, 119, 120, 123, 124 (bottom), 130/31, 145, 148 (both), 149 (top & bottom), 150 (left), 151 (right), 152, 153 (left top & left bottom), 161 (top), 164 (top left, top right & middle), 165 (top & bottom), 167 (bottom & inset), 169, 171, 177, 180 (bottom), 183.
Prado Museum: pages 6/7, 110/111.
South African Military Information Bureau: 17 (top), 100 (both).
TASS: page 57.
Terrorism Research Centre, South Africa: page 99 (inset).
HQ UK Land Forces: page 94 (bottom left & bottom right).
United Nations: pages 150/51 (bottom).
US Army: pages 41, 54/5, 55 (both), 59, 62 (bottom).
US Marines: pages 58 (both), 62 (top).
US Navy: pages 60/61.
US Signal Corps: pages 36/7 (inset).
Ivan D Yeaton College: pages 42 (bottom inset), 42/3.
Ruth Young: page 144.
Zionist Archive: page 142 (top).